News International took over —
Collins for £293 millions
and merged with Harper & Row
the knot 91 —

Harper Collins

Reed International bought —
Paul Hamlyn
Octopus

⅓ of Sinclair Stevenson (Imprint)

Terry Maher at Pentos, court
actions &
High courts

The Net Book Agreement
failed in 1996

BOOK COLLECTING

A · NEW · LOOK

BOOK COLLECTING
A · N E W · L O O K

ROY HARLEY LEWIS

David & Charles
Newton Abbot London North Pomfret (Vt)

British Library Cataloguing in Publication Data
Lewis, Roy Harley
  Book collecting: a new look.
  1. Book collecting
  I. Title
  002'.075   Z987

ISBN 0-7153-9025-2

Phototypeset by Northern Phototypesetting Co Bolton
Printed in Great Britain
by Billings & Sons Ltd Worcester
for David & Charles Publishers plc
Brunel House Newton Abbot Devon

Published in the United States of America
by David & Charles Inc
North Pomfret Vermont 05053 USA

CONTENTS

INTRODUCTION

It was inherent in the character of the essayist Michel de Montaigne (1533–92), to make sweeping statements for effect without bothering too much with the facts; he was an instinctive politician. So when he pronounced with his usual certainty: 'There are more books upon books than upon all other subjects', no one took him seriously enough to start counting. But for all his Gallic fondness for the dramatic flourish, de Montaigne had a point which has become more relevant over the centuries. Indeed, the trend has snowballed; scarcely a year elapses without another batch.

Apart from specialist studies, such as typography or binding, and anecdotal personal accounts of life in the bookworld, too many are concerned with what might be called the 'collecting for fun and profit' syndrome, reflecting the current preoccupation with prices. The surprising aspect of this steady output is that little has changed (apart, obviously, from fluctuating values) so that very few new books on the subject have very much to add to Andrew Block's *Book Collectors' Vade Mecum,* published in 1932 and setting the parameters for twentieth century collecting. Not only do many of the later works have limited life-cycles because of the changing fashions which influence prices, but their fascination with money debases the *raison d'etre* of collecting.

In normal circumstances the bibliophile will only sell a collection in the last resort, so that while it is important to be aware of current values when buying or selling, real satisfaction comes from the collecting process – the excitement of the chase, and each new discovery – not what the collection is worth in monetary terms. In other words, books – unlike model soldiers or postage stamps – are sought not only as artefacts, but for a variety of reasons . . . the

7

author or literary content . . . their value in research or the acquisition of knowledge . . . aesthetic considerations (the quality of paper, print and binding) . . . and even the link with the previous owners. A book may be desirable because of the way the collector relates to its special character – a reaction that is instinctive to the bibliophile, yet often beyond the comprehension of collectors in other fields. Obviously, it is reassuring for the bibliophile to know that after many years of scrimping and scraping, his books have become a tangible asset upon which his dependants could capitalise, but that is a bonus in afterthought, almost never the incentive.

It is also true that book enthusiasts indulge themselves and may not be above collecting 'rubbish' as they are tempted outside their specialist interests, but surely we are scraping the barrel when an otherwise commendable book collecting magazine publishes (as it did in 1985) a bibliography of Peter Cheyney's crime fiction, listing estimates for each of his titles, averaging £2–£3*. I'm not a literary snob, and have no objection to any person collecting any author or subject – but putting *price* tags on every book, irrespective of quality, reduces collecting to the level of buying groceries; it fosters a supermarket mentality worlds away from the passions that have fired bibliophiles to the most desperate measures . . . that, for example, drove the Spanish bookseller, Don Vincente, to arson and murder in retrieving beloved books he had been obliged to sell . . . or a more restrained Erasmus, three hundred years earlier, to declare: 'When I get a little money, I buy books; and if any is left I buy food and clothes.'

So why, having complained about the surfeit of books on collecting, am I offering another? It is simply a question of timing. The approach of the twenty-first century is an ideal cue for a reappraisal of collecting in the context of the bookworld in general, where significant changes already taking place encompass the whole spectrum from publishing through to the secondhand and antiquarian trade; we tend to forget that every trend or development in the different sectors has a knock-on effect.

This study is therefore concerned less with monetary values

---

*The relationship between £ and $ fluctuates from week to week, let alone over the years. In the absence of a precise figure, please reckon £1 to equal $1.20–$1.50.

(except, obviously, in the case of material of outstanding quality or interest), and more with an assessment of the changing patterns and their influence on the experienced collector. He or she will know, for example, about the importance of dust wrappers in relation to modern first editions, but probably not how this came about. Little has been written about dust jackets and their history, and the question of what to do with them is equally shrouded in mystery.

Book jackets are an integral part of the modern first yet the ephemera of yesterday – discarded by libraries and almost all collectors. But having discovered that the prudent does not throw *anything* away, there is a growing interest these days in ephemera as a subject in its own right, and a similar one in book plates. For different reasons, of course, the same applies to modern fine bindings.

Again, most books in the genre (including one of mine) have a chapter or two on the great collectors, but recently I have come to the conclusion that while we can take nothing away from these great achievements – society would be poorer without the philanthropy in this sense of men like J. Pierpoint Morgan and Sir Thomas Phillipps – there is nothing particularly clever about amassing vast and almost priceless libraries if you are a millionaire who can simply write a cheque for almost any amount, or even employ others to do the legwork.

Leaving aside the collecting 'giants', it can be argued that even a fairly rich person has to exercise control over his budget, possibly even weighing one purchase against another, but that is not the same as having to think twice before bidding for even modestly priced works. The great majority of us come into this category, knowing the frustration as our 'wants' lists get smaller and the remaining elusive titles more and more expensive, of having to let them go – in the bitter knowledge that if they ever appear again the price will be still higher! So I have chosen to turn the spotlight on a handful of interesting people who have had to rely on a degree of ingenuity, as well as knowledge of their subject and – a lot of patience.

Reference libraries are another neglected area. At a time when economic pressures affect the book trade across the board, many important libraries have had to stop buying anything more than essential new material (it being as much as they can afford to appropriate funds for keeping older books from falling to pieces), yet some still manage to do much more than merely mark time.

Most readers will take the phrase in the previous paragraph about books 'falling to pieces' with a pinch of salt, assuming that it was an exaggeration to make a point. But it was no mere figure of speech. While we have been preoccupied with our own collecting interests, books (paper and bindings) have been deteriorating at an accelerating rate. We are now faced with a *disease* that has been insidiously creeping up on us, almost unnoticed, and finally burst upon the bookworld – catching it almost unprepared. Gone are the days when libraries and institutional bodies regarded conservation as something they could get round to dealing with in some distant future when there was some spare cash around; today it is treated with as much urgency as the medical profession combats new and unexpected diseases, such as AIDS.

I hope that collectors on all levels will find something of interest in the chapters that follow, because the greater our awareness of the consequences of the upheaval taking place, the better equipped we shall be for consolidating our collecting interests, and for anticipating the ways in which they might be extended as well as safeguarded.

One

THE BOOK BUSINESS: AN UPDATE

It is said by those who should know, that the techniques of buying and selling are basically the same, whether we work for a multinational corporation or in a street market. Indeed, one successful American publisher is on record as saying that selling books is no different to selling shoes – and certainly no more creative. On the other hand, I used to know a man who sold lighthouses, and his working life was very different to that of any publisher or bookseller of my acquaintance.

But one thing is clear: books represent a volume turnover business, very different to others in that category such as carbon paper or drawing pins. You may wonder what 'volume turnover' has to do with collecting, but one forgets that the book trade – from publishing to retail outlet, through to dealer in secondhand and finally antiquarian books – is interdependent. This is not only because today's publication is obviously tomorrow's antiquarian book, but because the trading pattern of each stage directly affects the next, and so-on down the links of that chain. It is not possible to unravel this sometimes tangled web in logical sequence, but I'll try.

The link between publisher and collector is evident albeit indirect. In fiction, particularly, publishers consider themselves arbiters of taste, constantly unearthing the richest literary talent from which we should be able to satisfy our collecting interests. Unquestionably, the raw material is there to be mined, but publishing is a very hit and miss business, with some of our most gifted authors being unrecognised or even cold-shouldered at one time or another.

Think of children's literature and the name that springs to mind

11

is Hans Christian Andersen, yet his *Fairy Tales* were rejected by every publisher in Copenhagen, and eventually printed by himself. William Makepeace Thackeray's *Vanity Fair* did not 'fare' much better; the author being obliged to bring it out himself in monthly parts. Samuel Butler (1835–1902) whose talents were never appreciated in his lifetime had a particularly tough time with the two books for which he is best remembered – *Erewhon* (1872), brilliant by any standards yet turned down by his publisher and printed himself, and the very moving, *Way Of All Flesh*, which was published posthumously.

Even novels accepted for publication are not necessarily treated with any more respect. Jane Austen was paid £10 for *Northanger Abbey* by a Bath bookseller/publisher, who put it on one side for years, reluctant to venture into print and thus pour good money after bad! In more recent times there are many more examples, although the one that amuses me is *Day of the Jackal*, rejected so many times that Frederick Forsyth was on the point of giving up when it was taken up by a firm that had already given the thumbs down. I had a similar experience some years ago when a title rejected by one executive, was 're-claimed' by another in the same publishing house.

But today the noticeable difference is that economic factors force most publishers of fiction to cut down on the amount of 'inhouse' editing they are prepared to do. (In non-fiction, many 'farm out' much of the production work to specialist packaging companies.) The effect is that a number of very good 'manufactured' novels that arrived on the scene in the 1960s and 1970s are not being replaced, unless the author is already an established 'name' in whom the time invested has a guaranteed return. A typical example was the case of Peter Benchley, a talented American 'documentary' writer but initially short on experience of fiction. The publisher spotting the potential in his first major novel, made him re-write chunks, chapter by chapter, until the editor was happy – the result was *Jaws*. Nowadays, in most cases, the manuscript is either good enough to go into print without re-writes, or declined – because the turnover of titles has become more important.

Mention of *Jaws* reminds me of the author's namesake Robert Benchley, one of my favourite humorous writers, whose definition of talent, might have stood him in good stead as a publisher. 'It took me fifteen years to discover I had no talent for writing, but I couldn't give it up because by then I was too famous.' The point is that publishers, the first link in the chain, make mistakes; but then, so do we all.

Trading patterns at the end of the 1980s are changing more radically than at any time in a business which is not only affected by normal peaks and troughs, but further complicated and confused by sociological on top of economic factors. In relatively recent times – at least, since booksellers gave up their publishing activities – the retail outlet has been the fairly passive recipient of whatever the publisher had to offer. As this output multiplied, so competition for shelf-space increased, and with it the arrival of what became known as the 'non-book' (a typical example might be Princess X's diet/exercise/gardening diary). Film and TV tie-ins were another logical development; not just the story, but the story-behind-the-story and other promotional gimmicks, which have less and less to do with the traditional 'real' book.

But then the volume of new books began to get out of hand, affecting new and secondhand sectors. To quote Barry Shaw, publisher and editor of the weekly British trade journal, *Bookdealer*: 'At the peak of the recession in 1979 I predicted that many British book publishers would fail and that the annual number of new titles, around 42,000 and judged by most book-trade pundits as outrageously high, would fall. In fact, there have been very few failures and in 1986 publishers' output reached a record 57,845, an increase which probably has more to do with the desire to spread fixed costs across a larger number of books than any rise in demand from book buyers.

But if the present growth rate continues, there will be another million out-of-print titles for dealers in secondhand books to digest by the year 2000, almost doubling the size of the haystack in which book searchers must currently locate the desired needle. It will be a daunting task and whilst computerised stock control, with automatic print-out of reports will become widely used, it seems unlikely this will ever replace the human mind.'

I am sure Mr Shaw is right in anticipating a larger potential market for small dealers, or a larger slice of the cake for the larger, better organised firms, but from my experience the human brain will need to rely on the computer to an increasing extent, if only because the vast majority of dealers working alone conform to the traditional image of the person who loves books – and this to them means *literature*; to such people, science and technology are blind spots in which they will never develop an interest – despite the enormous and growing gap in the market.

But in predicting future trends it is easy to misinterpret the evidence. My motivation for writing the first *Book Browser's Guide to Secondhand & Antiquarian Bookshops* (David & Charles 1975) was a concern that the traditional 'browsers' bookshop was in danger of disappearing – forced out of business by escalating rents and rates, and replaced (especially in city centres) by building societies and banks – while, at the same time, the trade was actually expanding through the number of dealers selling through the mail. In other words, the bibliophile was still able to buy, but much of the pleasure – the opportunities to browse – were vanishing.

What I failed to take into consideration at the time was an element of naivety in the human make-up which inspires sober citizens (even ostensibly cautious accountants and lawyers) to imagine that a love of books (and varying degrees of knowledge) is sufficient qualification for running a bookshop. It meant that for every secondhand outlet that closed, another would open – sometimes destined to survive for a few years. So while the number of shops has been constant, the turnover remains high. Inevitably, a few more astute men and women succeed to join that small nucleus of outstanding secondhand bookstores that stay with us. But one would be hard-put to compile a list of fifty independent establishments (i.e. open to the public) with a good general stock of (say) over 30,000 titles, in the whole of the United Kingdom.

This balance is unlikely to change in the foreseeable future, unless the EEC's desire to 'harmonise' VAT throughout the European community eventually succeeds in overcoming the British Government's resistance, a second time round. The renewed threat is disturbing, because although booksales might dip only slightly before people become accustomed to the tax, it would spell the end of a number of small shops and dealers working from home who do not have the time, facilities or inclination to handle the administrative headaches involved. Larger businesses, particularly those who also sell stationery and other goods currently subject to the tax, are geared to cope with the additional workload, but few neighbourhood bookshops.

As soon as one moves 'upmarket' in search of better books, we become aware of the growing number of businesses getting rid of their shops, preferring to operate from showrooms behind closed doors. The movement which began in the United States but has spread to many countries in the West, has its origins in the need for greater security – the growing number of burglaries, as well as traditional shop-lifting – and economics, as rents for shop frontage in prime positions became exhorbitant. In the main, dealers who trade in more expensive books, are not interested in passing trade, having established a viable nucleus of customers who are prepared to call by appointment.

The trend may well be an inevitable consequence of the changes in society, but one of the unfortunate side-effects is that the customers for whom they are catering – before they could afford to buy expensive books – may well have developed taste and knowledge through browsing and selecting their purchases from substantial stocks with considerable care. Generations of young people in the professions and offices in major cities like London and New York would spend lunch-times browsing; today the same opportunities to develop an interest in old books has gone. Coupled with the accelerating competition directed at still younger groups from TV and home video, further inroads on reading habits are being made, especially on *what* is read. Publishers and some booksellers handling new publications may dispute the issue, quoting statistics given at the end of this chapter, but it is an inescapable fact that there are significant changes in reading habits and tastes, and that must have an effect on the collectors of tomorrow.

'Suitable' outlets are just one aspect of the problem of trying to keep abreast of events. Another is the volume of new titles, previously mentioned in a different context. Such mind-boggling statistics dull the palate, but let us just say that the figures are so large that in publishers' catalogues, reprints are generally listed in small print, and probably slip the attention of many booksellers, including the dealer in secondhand books. This means that certain out-of-print titles which have become expensive because of their scarcity, may lose much of their value overnight. While it does not apply to the modern 'first', it is frequently painful in cases of what might loosely be termed 'reference' works, where the edition is not usually as important as the content – provided that the reprint has maintained the same production standards. There are numerous examples, but one that springs to mind is the three books on Georgian country houses by Christopher Hussey, originally published by Country Life. The three titles, *Early, Mid* and *Late Georgian Houses,* were important studies, attractively produced, and once out-of-print became increasingly difficult to find outside bigger libraries. At one stage fine copies were fetching around £100 (each title) which meant that when the Antiques Collectors' Club reprinted the series a few years later at £20 per volume, dealers who had purchased the original editions at inflated prices had the bottom knocked out of that market. That is only one title, admittedly, but repeated enough times, it becomes more than a source of irritation.

The cost paring policies of most British and American publishers in the last quarter of the century, i.e. hedging bets by increasing the number of titles but reducing print runs to a minimum, may seem to be justified by overall sales figures, but may well be a short-sighted policy – quite apart from the cost to the secondhand trade, let alone authors! Leaving aside the tiny proportion of automatic best sellers, by the time the merits of a particular book (not considered worthy of a 'hype' promotion) has been spread by word of mouth, it may already be out-of-print. A further run is no longer automatic; publishers might feel confident of selling the extra copies, but are obliged to weigh the substantial cost of an immediate investment in paper, print and binding against the uncertain return on sales over an indeterminate period – funds that might be better invested in other areas.

However, there are many examples on both sides of the Atlantic, particularly in fiction which generally has a faster sales cycle, where publishers have failed to capitalise on excellent reviews, to reprint potential best sellers while interest is still fresh – so cautious have they become. Meanwhile, secondhand prices will rise (and profit margins) with the growing demand for a diminishing number of out-of-print copies, which sounds fine from the booksellers' point of view – until he has laid in a small stock at the higher prices, and the book is unexpectedly reprinted, either by the original publisher, or another specialising in library supplies.

Much the same applies to remainders, which further confuse the market and book prices. Once, a far sighted secondhand bookseller could order certain new titles in the knowledge that once out-of-print, there will be a fresh demand. But publishers influenced by periodic cash-flow problems are tempted to remainder excellent books which (certainly from the author's standpoint) merit the published price. Because of the growth in specialist remainder shops we tend to think of them as another feature of society's surrender to built-in obsolescence, yet they were, in fact, pioneered two hundred years ago by a London bookseller, James Lackington, who resisted the practice of destroying half or even three quarters of leftover stock in order to charge full price on what was left. Lackington upset the trade by selling such stock at a fraction of the retail price, and by reaching a wider public helped boost book sales generally. In 1791 he estimated that four times the number of books were being sold as had been twenty years before.

Remainders are usually excellent value and if a book has any merit at all, the chances are that it will appreciate as soon as stocks disappear. One of the earliest examples was the two-volume *Some Account of the English Stage 1660–1830,* by the Rev. John Genest, published in 1832 at £5.5s (£5.25), and remaindered at one fifth of that price; today it is worth several hundred pounds. This has nothing to do with bad judgement on the part of the publisher; if anyone understood book values, it was Bernard Quaritch (1819–99), founder of the London antiquarian booksellers of that name. Yet Quaritch, the greatest bookseller who ever lived (if you believe his obituaries) got cold feet when he published an Edward Fitzgerald translation of the *Rubaiyat of Omar Khayyam* in 1859 in an edition limited to 250 copies, and was stuck with the bulk of them. Cutting his losses, he remaindered them at one (old) penny each. The irony of this anecdote is that the firm recouped his losses in 1979 from the sale of just one of those copies. Mind you, it had to fork out £4,620 in the process!

Any reference to the Omar Khayyam always makes me wonder if there is not something a trifle weird about this book, even a hoodoo on it. The magnificent Sangorski and Sutcliffe binding of the large Vedder edition – probably the finest decorated leather binding ever created (the decoration included 1051 semi-precious jewels plus an emerald representing a snake's eye on the *inside* of the front cover), went down with the Titanic in 1912. Six weeks later Frank Sangorski, at the age of thirty-seven, was drowned in a bathing accident, and within another few months one of his assistants was also dead. In the 1930s the same firm spent seven years reproducing the masterpiece from the original drawings – only to lose it when London was bombed in World War II.

Meanwhile, the face of the trade in new books has also been changing; surprising success being achieved by relative newcomers – in the main, shrewd businessmen who happen to like books, as opposed to their predecessors who were bookmen with an aptitude for business. Such new retail outlets may, through rapid expansion eventually restore the power and influence of the bookseller.

An outstanding example is Terry Maher's rapidly growing Pentos group, which has the relaunched Dillon's bookshop in London as its flagship, impressively supported by two of the better names of the bookworld, Hudson's of Birmingham and Weatherhead's of Aylesbury, heading a group of 35 large conventional bookselling outlets – and more than 50 Athena shops and galleries, specialising in cards, prints and posters, but already selling a growing number of books. The company's aim is to have 250 Athena outlets within the next five years, further 'traditional' bookshops, and even an expanded operation in the USA.

Yet what impresses most is not the size of this programme but the comprehensiveness of the marketing philosophy, affecting every aspect of the selling cycle. 'In every other trade it is the retail market that calls the tune,' maintains Terry Maher, 'yet in the bookworld, traditionally the publisher has had all the power and shops get what is offered. Our marketing strategy is successful enough to change the balance.'

Dillons had always been among the top half dozen bookshops in the United Kingdom, but cramped to some extent by their reputation for specialising in academic material, an image perpetuated by the earlier name Dillons *University* Bookshop – a legacy of the days when it was a joint-venture operation with the University of London. Pentos bought the business in 1977, but the £1.5M restructuring and refurbishing programme did not take place until nine years later to coincide with the shop's fiftieth anniversary.

Despite Dillon's long established reputation, its position near the University is slightly off the beaten track, and since management's intention was to bring it to the attention of the 'new' potential book-buyer, the opening was the occasion to launch an advertising campaign, which by its aggressiveness broke new ground in this normally conservative field. Typical was a poster sited near Foyles, their principal rival in London, announcing: 'Foiled Again? Try Dillons.' The few lines of sales blurb concluded, 'Europe's finest bookstore is at . . .' It must be more than a coincidence that sales figures during the early weeks of the 'new' shop were approaching 30% up on the same period in the previous year.

It is a fact that the book trade has always been somewhat amateurish; putting books on display, no matter how attractively arranged, in the hope of attracting sales is just the start – the scope for 'exploitation' is much greater. The Pentos approach has been to recognise a separate market, back to back with the traditional outlets for serious book buyers. This is aimed at a much wider cross section of society, but concentrated on the young by creating through the Athena group of shops and galleries an upbeat environment where books can be sold to people who would not normally go into a bookshop; an atmosphere built on pop music and images, using light, colour and sound to create an air of 'excitement' associated more with retail clothes outlets attracting the young. This is a new and very large untapped market, particularly interesting in view of the normally very low ratio of customers and browsers to actual sales.

Very little market research on book buying has been done, but a small survey conducted a few years ago in the UK, sampling 3,000 people in 51 shops, discovered that only 33% actually bought anything, and of these 45% acted on impulse. While I have always been somewhat sceptical of polls and surveys, from my own observations over many years those figures ring true, and that would seem to leave considerable scope for the environment to be more sales orientated and for sales staff to be more effectively employed. The mass market for greeting cards, posters, stationery and records, for example, has never been explored by publishers, and the Pentos experience is that by selecting titles carefully (stocking relatively few in this type of venue, compared with ten times the number in one of the very large traditional bookshops) they are reaching a youthful audience new to reading books and who may be weaned from those on (say) pop music or sport to broader areas of interest.

The advantage of size – being able to buy more competitively is just one factor – is obvious, but there is much more to running any business, and the most talented people can come unstuck. One man who, more than any other in the 1960s, made people aware of secondhand books and who put a hitherto unknown little Welsh town on the map, was 'King' Richard Booth. The town which, within a few years, became the world's only tourist centre for bibliophiles, is Hay-on-Wye, and Booth's title (Richard Coeur de Livres) was self-bestowed in 1977 when he declared the town independent of the British Isles!

Like many strong personalities, Booth had a number of critics, but what he accomplished in twenty years was quite remarkable. His basic philosophy was to remove the mystique from bookselling; and operate on a huge scale by employing sensible, yet then quite novel marketing techniques. Having settled on Hay-on-Wye because of its easy access from major cities like Birmingham, Bristol, and other heavily populated catchment areas, he began taking over the town – one of his early purchases, the local cinema, entered the *Guinness Book of Records* as the world's largest secondhand bookshop with the somewhat controversial claim of one million books on 8.5 miles of shelving. With such innovative ideas as subsidised day-return coach trips from London, and free overnight accommodation for librarians, sales boomed; his success attracting other booksellers, so that eventually even the general public were talking about the famous town of books. But after twenty years, for various reasons, Booth's vast operation began to disintegrate, and he was forced to sell off unit after unit. Nevertheless, I shall be surprised if a person of such ability, dynamism, and 'feel' for books, does not eventually come back in style.

The man who took over the Cinema Bookshop in Hay, and subsequently two other Booth outlets in the same town, Leon Morelli of the Pharos Distribution Services company, whose experience of books had been virtually restricted to their despatch to all parts of the world, is another who believes in the benefits of operating on a grand scale. The basic difference is that Morelli's shops in different parts of the country endeavour to retain their individual characters. The twelve in what became known as the Quintos group, include such respected names as Francis Edwards, in London's Marylebone High Street (purpose-built in 1911, although the firm was launched with that name in 1855), and Reads (formerly Joseph's) of Charing Cross Road; that site dating from 1902; Commins of Bournemouth, and Jean Pain of Cambridge; as well as smaller specialist businesses.

In common with most trades, bookselling has always been dominated by a handful of businesses or individuals; each having made a conscious decision on which market sector they would concentrate. I know of one, for example, who even has something in common with my lighthouse salesman – selling fewer and fewer but successively more valuable books, and aiming at an eventual target of no more than a half-dozen exceptional items in any one year. Between such highlights he keeps his hand in by buying books and fine bindings that will give him collecting satisfaction – before selling (at a profit) at a later date.

At the other end of the scale is Paul Minet, another trend-setter who derives much of his satisfaction from exploring new concepts in bookselling. Essentially a book person (he took his first subscription to the *Clique*, long established British trade weekly, at the age of fifteen), Minet is very much a person of ideas disciplined by a natural business acumen. Having trained as a journalist, he was soon drawn by the bookworld, and founded the *Antiquarian Book Monthly Review* in 1977, editing it for a while, and remaining a contributor. Coming from a talented family, and inheriting a wealth of entrepreneurial skills and drive, he decided early on that to operate on an ambitious scale would make him a big fish in a relatively small pond. Learning the practicalities of the trade in the West Country, and inspired by what Richard Booth was doing at Hay-on-Wye, he moved to London's West End where he opened a couple of attractive conventional shops, and finally a third in a very smart location – the World of Books – the nearest approach to a book supermarket I have encountered; at least, it operated on the same principle but without the hygenic gloss, although no one cared about the bare boards because of the enormous range of modestly priced stock amongst which they could browse. The World of Books was very much a 'one-off' and it was a loss to collectors when the lease expired, and to renew would have meant a trebling of the rent and a reduction in space; it closed.

Meanwhile, having moved to East Sussex where he bought the wing of a country house, with an abundance of space for books, another person might have been tempted to ease down and operate from home by catalogue. But Minet needs an outlet for his restless energy, and coupled with a concern for his assistants, he decided to start again. Knowing that property in Central London was prohibitively expensive, and rents in the more attractive provincial towns not much better, he looked for a place that did not yet have the status of a Bath, Guildford, or York, but had the potential tourist appeal to be nudged in that direction. He settled on little known Rochester, in Kent, an old Roman city he had 'discovered' when the French hospital for Huguenots, founded in 1708, of which he had been a director for many years, moved its alms houses there from East London. The main attractions were its proximity to three major motorways, and the fact that rents, although rising, were still very favourable compared to London – which was very much nearer than Hay-on-Wye, to some extent his model.

Stage one of the plan was the opening of two shops in the High Street; the World of Books (more a note of nostalgia than an indication of size), and Baggins, much bigger, and site of a novel 'Storage With Dividends' scheme. Unlike the traditional 'shop-within-a-shop' concept, in which individual dealers pay rent for space and additional facilities, this scheme is even simpler, and without any financial commitment. Every book on show bears the dealer's pencilled price and initials. Sales are recorded in a computerised cash register giving a daily print out, and participating dealers receive fortnightly cheques for 70% of the sales value; all overheads – including Minet's staff – being covered by the remaining 30%. Initially 4,500 square feet of space was shared between his stock and that of ten dealers, but the proportion shrank with the arrival of each newcomer, so that by the end of 1987 the place was full, twenty individual dealers were represented on site, offering 250,000 books – a small waiting list necessitating the need for further shop space.

'Pooling overheads in this way is attractive to booksellers,' Minet maintains. 'Running a small bookstore is a high risk business; apart from rents and rates, the individual needs to turnover his stock which means he should employ someone while he looks, and that probably represents an annual turnover of £40,000–£50,000. Book fairs are an alternative, but many find they cannot shift enough that way, and this offers a half-way point between having a shop, and operating at fairs.'

As his proportion of the stock in Baggins went down Minet opened a third outlet, Piccadilly Rare Books, specialising in travel and military books. But meanwhile, the old part of the town was being renovated and it seems inevitable that, like the original Booth operation at Hay-on-Wye, he will attract other booksellers to open their own shops in Rochester. His early advertising in magazines like *Country Life* and *In Britain* reads like a prediction: 'Visit Rochester for its Norman castle, Norman cathedral, 38 restaurants, specialist shops – and secondhand bookshops.' Names were not necessary.

Returning to the antiquarian sector, the most evident changes, following a trend started in the United States, has been the move away from shop premises to operating by appointment from behind closed doors. Another has been the increasing number of take-overs and mergers, inevitable in a high capital business where a number of old established companies have secured the backing of the City, institutional bodies, or 'outside' directors. One 'new look' London operation which seems to have benefitted from both trends is what is now known as E. Joseph in association with Charles J. Sawyer, both distinguished names on the English antiquarian scene, firms with fascinating histories in their own right.

The families' relationship dates back to the 1870s when a thriving secondhand bookshop in Holywell Street, then London's centre for old books was run by a Mrs Lazarus who employed some bright young assistants who went on to make their own names, among them her nephew Emmanuel Joseph and Charles Sawyer. Although the family is descended from a long line of booksellers, Joseph's did not trade under that name until 1902 when young Emmanuel started the exodus from Holywell Street to the new bookselling Mecca, Charing Cross Road – an intriguing precedent for his great-grandson, David Brass, who gave up the famous Charing Cross Road corner site only a few years ago when the character of the business changed, in keeping with the times, from basically general secondhand to fine, rare books; and he moved to third floor premises in Vere Street. Charles Sawyer's business was established in 1894 when, as a young assistant he had the good fortune to impress a retired American bookdealer, who offered to back a West End venture. It was his grandson, Richard who in 1986 gave up the shop in Grafton Street to join forces with David Brass.

The two men, both just forty, and having learned the trade and its ethics from packing upwards (the reader who wonders what there is to learn about packing, has obviously never suffered the experience of buying from the new breed of bookseller who think nothing of mailing books unprotected in a large envelope), typify the changing image of the antiquarian bookseller from that of a stooping octogenarian to jetsetter. Almost imperceptibly, faces in the sales rooms on both sides of the Atlantic are getting younger, and the change coincides with the separation of the general secondhand and antiquarian sectors where the dividing line is now far less blurred. More and more antiquarian dealers are moving away from the middle ground, to concentrate on the best material they can obtain. Because of greater demand for fine books, and greater awareness among collectors, the days when provincial booksellers were happy to offer their 'special' books to the London firms are gone. Today the better dealers go looking – which usually means abroad. Brass and Sawyer reckon to each separately spend twelve weeks in a year abroad (both in the United States, and Brass also in Japan), buying, selling and making new contacts.

Despite the company's forward looking policy, supported by computer systems and other modern 'tools' of the trade, its business philosophy is traditional, regarding its dealings with the public as a two-way relationship. This is helped by the decision to continue in the areas in which both firms built their reputation, i.e. fine and rare books, private press and colour plate books, sets and fine bindings. 'People know us for what we do well,' says Richard Sawyer. 'There will always be a market for our type of stock. It is not our job to speculate on what books might be collected tomorrow. I see our role more as servants of our customers than to tell them what they should be collecting.'

Of course, the so-called 'top end' of the market is not exclusively antiquarian at a time when modern first editions with dust wrappers, or proof copies, can fetch four figure amounts. How long this boom will last (as more relatively recent copies surface) remains to be seen, but for the immediate future it remains a very buoyant sector, ranging from run-of-the-mill to the very special rare titles in fine condition – the accent being on the word 'fine' because condition makes all the difference when a collector might reject a dust jacket with even the slightest nick. In this latter category prices are obviously dictated by condition (coupled with scarcity) because dealers have to be prepared to pay over-the-odds to get the most desirable items. As in the case of antiquarian books where, usually, the outstanding dealers have been those who had the courage to gamble on their judgement, so a handful of specialists in modern literature have come to the fore in recent years. Rick Gekoski, one such specialist trading on both sides of the Atlantic, is an American academic living in England where he operates from bases in Leamington Spa and London.

Coming to bookselling after fourteen years as a lecturer in English literature at the universities of Oxford and Warwick, Gekoski offset his lack of business experience with the academic's special knowledge of modern writers and their work. Many of us are familiar with the writings of literary giants such as Evelyn Waugh and Graham Greene, but would be hard-put to remember the order in which the books were published, the background to each title and the circumstances in which they were written or commissioned. Indeed, Gekoski does not regard the two apparently dissimilar careers as unrelated, because he is still working in an environment he loves. His in-depth study of authors, and their relationships with each other has given him an awareness of the availability of manuscript material and even correspondence unknown to most dealers. Coupled with his own collecting interests, it enabled him to know instinctively which material was really scarce and which was relatively commonplace. Linked to this knowledge, his willingness to pay unprecedented prices to get the choicest items, enabled him to build a reputation in the trade within a couple of years.

Gekoski's own collecting these days is limited to William Golding and association copies (in this case, obviously of a literary nature, e.g. one celebrated author's dedication to another), but he derives an element of creative satisfaction from his own private printing press, The Sixth Chamber Press, with the fine quality of production one would expect; in fact, designed by Sebastian Carter of the better known Rampant Lions Press. Again, his background has enabled him to approach 'name' authors who might not normally be associated with limited edition material. He began by publishing William Golding's Nobel Prize lecture, and followed with some short stories of John Updike, and works by Gavin Ewart, Peter Redgrave, D. M. Thomas and Paul Theroux.

By restricting one's activity to a narrow area of interest, such as modern firsts, a dealer can operate without conventional business premises, although access to shelf space in a retail outlet can be useful. But the bookseller moving up the ladder in the wider field of antiquarian books is faced with greater problems. Long established firms generally have large reserves of stock, and may own their premises, or have favourable leases (either of which may have been made possible in the past by major injections of capital).

As life becomes progressively tougher for all but the most efficient, there is an increasing element of competition from the larger auction houses – the growing practice of handling private sales incurring no little jealousy among booksellers. It was Sotheby's, for example, who represented the owner of the Murthy Book of Hours (see Chapter 5) sold to the National Library of Scotland in 1986, having been asked to find a suitable buyer prior to auction. Having ascertained interest they granted the National Library a six-month period in which to raise the money. Auction houses who have large institutional bodies among their regular clients say that if asked to handle such transactions they cannot refuse. And the gap narrows as, in normal business, most auction houses are these days prepared to advance a substantial portion of the estimated price, so that vendors no longer have to wait several months for their money.

To the dismay of a few of their members, the Antiquarian Booksellers Association adopts a 'free-market' policy. Senga Grant, current President of the ABA, says: 'There is room for both of us, as there always has been. The auction houses will continue to attract major collections, and I personally feel that in these days of vast capital needs for acquisition, the auction gives all of us the opportunity to select and purchase within our specialist fields.'

However, to return to the younger bookseller wishing to move to better premises, or to substantially improve the quality of stock, the headache is one of capital; borrowing from traditional sources can be restrictive as well as expensive. One such avenue which opened up in the 1970s and 1980s to the candidate who could offer the right blend of energy and experience, backed by a good trading record, was explored by Robert Frew and Julian Mackenzie, who had run the Primrose Hill Bookshop, Hampstead, since 1977. The shop, dealing in general secondhand books, was healthy enough, but the partners agreed that they had progressed as far as they could at that location. Deciding to concentrate on 'better' books, they were drawn like Dick Whittington to Central London – which (apart from the greater volume of shops) offers such incentives as book auctions every week in the season. But decent premises in a prime spot – they ended up in Great Russell Street, a couple of minutes walk from the British Library and right opposite the TUC building, in itself a crowd-puller – plus the acquisition of new stock, meant very considerable additional resources. They approached the Government's Business Expansion Scheme, set up to help small businesses gain access to 'risk' capital.

The concept of BES is to encourage people with substantial (i.e. highly taxed) incomes, to invest in selected businesses, with the attraction of tax concessions. The financial complexities of these negotiations would tax the brain of an accountant and since we are concerned merely with broad principles, suffice to say that with the Primrose Hill shop still operating under a manager as part security, Frew Mackenzie opened for trading in 1986, with a 'cushion' of £420,000 free of interest for three years – terms that make the banks seem like robber barons. Because the scheme had been abused by companies concerned more with accumulating assets than trading and generating employment, the regulations have been tightened, although that should not prevent genuine booksellers from applying if they want to move in that direction. However, whether potential shareholders can be persuaded that a bookshop is the best way in which to invest their money these days (see Chapter 3) is another matter.

The future of Frew Mackenzie, and others following along this path, depends to a great extent on the ability to turn over stock in the £50–£5,000 range, supported by a mailing list which will undoubtedly grow as they reach their target of six to nine catalogues a year. The problem may be less in selling than in acquiring the quality of stock they seek in sufficient quantities –

but then, that is what bookselling is all about.

The ABA's attitude towards public funding is somewhat cautious. Mrs Grant comments: 'In the main, private sources will continue to provide the backbone of capital. This trade has always had its traditions and traditionalists, and I see nothing wrong in that as it has never blinded us to opportunities both in the home and world markets.'

Statistics, because of the way they are assembled, do not necessarily give a complete picture, but three recent reports on the British book scene by the ICC Information Group – the Key Note Marketing Report on Booksellers, the ICC Business Ratio Report on Publishers, and the Industrial Performance Analysis 1986/87 – make encouraging reading for the new book sector at least. Home sales rose £70M to £720M in 1985 – total sales rising 34.3% over the three-year period to 1985. Figures like these surprisingly put publishing at the head of the industry table for high profits, high returns on investment and shareholder funds, and the best rate of growth for capital employed, over the previous three years.

The IPA report does point out that the expansion in publishing (as well as in consumer services) should be viewed in conjunction with the decline of more traditional manufacturing in Britain; in other words, as we have always suspected, people tend to read more in a bid for escapism during 'difficult' periods. The same study goes on to suggest that the first quarter's figures for 1986 when general trading profits fell sharply, indicate a 'plateau effect' for the immediate future.

I have no quarrel with any air of optimism, but it should be kept in perspective; another report at about the same time from Dun and Bradstreet revealed that business failures across the board in the paper, print and publishing industry in England and Wales in the first six months of 1986 totalled 315 – a rise of 8.6% on the same period in 1985; a cautionary note when one might be dazzled by publishers' profit margins. In any case it seems likely that the number of publishing houses will contract over the next few years.

The still rising output of new books is so great that although major booksellers and chains have expanded their operations to keep pace, a significant slice of the market is being taken by retail outlets outside the trade, such as supermarkets and petrol stations, while publishers like Mills and Boon, specialists in romantic fiction, have even experimented with bingo halls. Admittedly, most of these books are paperbacks, which is probably where the future of fiction publishing lies – the rest mainly 'non-books' – but so long as they are being sold it does not much matter where. If the reading habit can be revived at the lowest level, there is the possibility that 'new' readers will graduate to other books. One can only hope, however, that by then 'real' books have not been replaced in the bookshops by audio and video cassettes which are already gaining a foothold in the United States, under the disarming guise of 'story-telling'. If children are induced to sit in front of a TV screen to watch a personable actor read the classics of literature, what incentive is there for them to learn to read for themselves? Still, I suppose much the same fear was expressed when comics were first introduced and there are few collectors around today who were not once avid readers of comics.

Two

IN QUEST OF THE PERFECT BOOK

Beauty lies in the eye of the beholder, so we are led to believe. It is certainly true that we have our own views on what constitutes the 'perfect' or, better say the 'ideal' book. I've borrowed the chapter heading from a work written in 1926 by William Dana Orcut, an American printer of impeccable taste (which means, I suppose, that it conforms with mine), who in picking up an out-of-the-ordinary volume would look first at the type-face, the quality of the ink, and even the amount of white space, before he got round to the words. Orcut was an historian and connoisseur of print who opened many eyes to a feature of book production that many were inclined to overlook.

But such considerations are only part of the story. As I said at the outset, we may lust after a book for so many different reasons – beauty, content, even its associations – but once singled out and put under the spotlight, it seems to acquire an aura – a translucent *glow* of such magical properties that it transcends objectivity; unique features are absorbed to become an integral part of the whole. Over the years, I have been fortunate enough to examine a number of sixteenth and even fifteenth century works, including a couple of Caxton's, and I can remember each experience with almost total recall, as though I had been given access to the Crown jewels.

Such books are the stuff of dreams. Few of us ever aspire to owning anything truly outstanding; masterpieces possessing the qualities that break sales-price records, invariably end up in a museum or library. However, not everything in the Super Book League necessarily costs a fortune – although why is it *we* never seem to hear about them until it's too late? It may be of modest origins – perhaps even something once remaindered. Anyone whose interest is confined to prices should stop reading at this point, and switch to Book Auction Records, which I can highly recommend, if you like that sort of thing.

By dreams, I am talking about the *romance* of books and collecting; the treasure in the attic, the other fellow's good fortune – the stories that capture our imagination, filling us with such awe that we are able to contemplate them without envy, in much the same way that the general public seems to regard its soap opera heroes and heroines.

The person who does not collect – in other words, the emotionally deprived soul – could not comprehend the depth of our feelings when it comes to the very special book. The incidents of arson and murder reported earlier may seem a little 'over the top', and in any case, happened in less civilised times, but there are a number of more down-to-earth stories to prove the point. The one that sticks in my memory is about the affluent farmer from America's Midwest who was an avid collector, and whose library by the time of his death was worth a small fortune. To whom did he bequeath the collection? *Not* to family, or special friends – but to his bookseller! The legacy was in memory of countless hours of happiness received from the books obtained for him! (I have tried very hard, without success, to substantiate the truth of this anecdote – which is very different to a number of authenticated cases of dealers being given first option to buy back material on a customer's death – so you will have to take it on trust.) Unfortunately, other stories I do know to be true are rather dull, and you would not thank me for recording them.

While the average person fantasises about winning a big sweepstake or state lottery, the bibliophile thinks in terms of Boadicea's long lost battle orders, or the personal diary of Queen Elizabeth I with, of course, irrefutable proof of their authenticity. In 1981 I wrote a crime novel *The Manuscript Murders,* about the speculation surrounding a hitherto unknown journal written by Emilia Lanier, identified to the satisfaction of most by Dr A. L. Rowse as the Dark Lady of Shakespeare's *Sonnets.* Expert advice confirmed my belief that a handwritten forgery laboriously carried out by a person with sufficient skill, and knowledge of the period, probably would remain undetected – short of laboratory tests; these were unlikely to be carried out, except in the case of something really sensational, such as a new play by Shakespeare. The reason is that if the provenance can be established, and the evidence seems acceptable, we *want* the discovery to be genuine!

However, when it comes to Shakespeare – apart from the exceptional talent – his style, speech rhythms and word patterns are so well known that the forger attempting to create something new, does not stand a chance; there is no need even to consult the scientists. Since the Bard's death, approaching ninety plays attributed to him have failed to stand up to closer examination, yet we continue to live in hope that one day . . . The obvious places have been tried, so there is little point in prising up the floorboards of Ann Hathaway's cottage, or breaking into Shakespeare's tomb. But in 1985, Gary Taylor, a young American scholar, found an unknown ninety-line, nine stanza poem in Oxford's Bodleian Library – and which, on the assumption it is genuine, was the first new work found this century. If the discovery was stunning to Taylor and the literary world, it should not be to those of us who have always been convinced that the obvious place to lose or hide a book is in a library, and recall that in 1976 a Belfast schoolmaster, Colin McKelvie, found a first edition of *Gulliver's Travels* (1726), with copious and important alterations made by Jonathan Swift, who had apparently only just seen the first printed copy – in a public library!

Taylor, joint general editor of the revised and expanded Oxford University Press *Complete Works of Shakespeare,* was doing some cross-checking of early manuscript material shortly before going to press, when he opened an anthology of English Renaissance poetry, probably compiled in the 1630s, twenty years after Shakespeare's death. The identity of the seventeenth-century writer or 'editor' is not known, but he had attributed two poems to 'William Shakespeare'; one which Taylor immediately recognised, the other unknown to him. Having studied the poem, he had an instinctive feeling it was genuine, but was cautious enough to take the view that his opinion, even as an authority on the subject, did not matter so much as the fact the *compiler* believed it..The volume had been in the Bodleian since 1756, as part of a bequest of hundreds of books and manuscripts from a graduate of St. John's College, Oxford, Richard Rawlinson, a well known bibliophile.

Deliberately setting out to *disprove* his theory, Gary Taylor first established the anthology itself was genuine, and that the passage had not been added at a later date. Although the style was unremarkable by comparison with other Shakespearian poetry (which is usually the main objection of those who remain unconvinced by anything that might be new), Taylor used a computerised dictionary to analyse the way words had been used. It is not disputed that Shakespeare had the largest vocabulary of any writer in the English language, and frequently employed words not used elsewhere, yet it was found that the poem contained almost 100 phrases that bore similarities to passages in his other works. Furthermore, the rhyme pattern (one rhyme for every three syllables), led Taylor and his supporters to the belief it might have been written by a young poet still developing his style, and that it might have been composed some ten to fifteen years before his established poetry.

The majority of Elizabethan scholars now accept the poem, although in itself of minor importance, is genuine. Others will never be convinced, any more than will those who maintain that the Bard's works were written by Bacon, Marlowe, or anyone else. Indeed the correspondence between scholars in the *Times Literary Supplement* went on for weeks, with points scored on both sides. In comparison, my own knowledge of the subject is too flimsy to offer a constructive opinion, except to say: why *shouldn't* it be the real thing?! Someone who does have the expertise is Dr John Pitcher of St. John's College who in supporting Gary Taylor's findings is quoted as saying: 'Some people will not be satisfied unless Shakespeare himself reaches out of the grave and signs it.'

To read the poem in updated English, you will need a copy of the OUP Shakespeare, but as an appetiser, here is the first stanza:

> Shall I die? Shall I fly
> Lovers' baits and deceits,
> > sorrow breeding?
> Shall I fend Shall I send?
> Shall I shew, and not rue
> > my proceeding?
> In all duty her beauty
> Binds me her servant for ever.
> If she scorn, I mourn
> I retire to despair, joying never.

Among Elizabethan dramatists, most authorities consider John Webster second only to Shakespeare, but because he was not as prolific (and his two remarkable plays, *The Duchess of Malfi* and *The White Devil* are somewhat similar in mood), there is less positive evidence of a Webster style, and recognisable features such as plot construction, vocabulary and his use of words – which means that it is more difficult to authenticate anything new that might be attributed to him. It is this difficulty which seems to have been the stumbling block to an abortive London sale in 1986 of a working draft of a previously unrecorded tragedy by Webster.

Bloomsbury Book Auctions, handling the sale on behalf of the Trustees of the Melbourne Garden Charities (i.e. Melbourne Hall in Derbyshire), were sufficiently convinced to produce a special catalogue for this one lot, describing the manuscript as 'one of the most exciting literary discoveries of the century'. The catalogue features photographs of what are described as the only existing examples of Webster's handwriting. Found at Melbourne Hall, the manuscript was probably written between 1606 and 1609, and consists of four heavily corrected pages, approximately one scene of a tragedy based on the story of Alessandro dei Medici, Duke of Florence, who was murdered by his kinsman Lorenzo dei Medici; it is possibly the only surviving 'foul' paper, or playwright's draft from the period.

The Webster manuscript had been preserved among the papers of Sir John Coke, Secretary of State to Charles I, and his descendants at Melbourne Hall, for 350 years. There is evidence to suggest it had probably been used as wrapping paper when Sir John's books and papers were sent from Gray's Inn to Derbyshire in 1634, and as such surprisingly not thrown away at some stage.

The catalogue presents an impressive case in maintaining the manuscript's authenticity, drawing comparisons with passages in *The White Devil* and *The Duchess of Malfi*, and quoting Graham Greene, from *British Dramatists*, London 1942: '. . . Alone among these men he left behind something essentially his: only a scholar could differentiate between untitled scraps of the other poets, but Webster's tone is unmistakeable – the keen, economical, pointed oddity of the dialogue – whether in prose or verse – expressing the night side of life . . .' Confidently, the auction house estimated the price it would fetch as between £200,000–£400,000.

The only feasible explanation for the failure of the manuscript to sell is that there was insufficient time between its discovery at Melbourne Hall, and the sale (possibly prompted by the need to raise money for the upkeep of the garden – the only surviving Queen Anne garden in England), for the 'experts' to debate the issue in the usual way; that could have meant that bidders were unhappy about committing themselves to such large sums of money until it had been accepted as genuine Webster. No doubt it will turn up again in due course.

At about the same time, another important manuscript with Shakespearian associations – this time in the form of a water-stained, vellum-bound notebook bearing the date 1594, was discovered at the back of an underclothes drawer! No one remembers how it got there (in all probability, just to get it out of the way), although by a little stretch of the imagination it *could* have been inherited as the family's history goes back to pre-Elizabethan days. Because the contemporary handwriting was difficult to decipher it was taken to Sotheby's.*[1] Experts in the manuscript department, consulting with Elizabethan scholars, concluded that the notebook – containing hurried notes taken during a performance of King Henry IV, Part I, and subsequently 'polished' from memory – represented the earliest substantial examples of quotations from Shakespeare, taken at a time when his genius had not yet been generally accepted. Although the writer's identity is not known, the implication is that he was a discerning playgoer who may have made a hobby of collecting quotations from the works of the many talented Elizabethan writers. His notes would have preceded the play in printed form, so it does not stretch the imagination to picture him as a collector setting a precedent for today's interest in pre-published material! The handwriting conforms to the style associated with the 1590s, while an alteration to Shakespeare's text on a specific point, indicates that the notes must have been made before the death of Queen Elizabeth in 1603; more positive, however, is the fact that a large section of Latin notes on metaphysical subjects written in the same hand in the rest

*Since so many of the most exciting books only come to light through public auction, from which many of these examples are taken, it may be an entertaining challenge for readers to try and guess the prices attained, so these are listed in numerical order at the end of the chapter.

of the book, is dated 1594.

The discovery of the manuscript is of major importance to historians because the quotations are the first known actual reconstruction of a play by Shakespeare from notes and memory – an idea which obviously caught on from the number of later examples produced by actors and printers, or others who pirated play texts, e.g. certain of the Quartos. In this case, the writer made rough headings, suggesting that he planned to produce a more 'elegant' version, and they provide the best and possibly the earliest example of the contemporary use of one of the plays as material for a commonplace book; indeed, the earliest known substantial excerpt of any kind from one of Shakespeare's plays. Dating from early in his writing career, that it was done at all indicates that his reputation was already spreading. The successful bidder was the British Library.

Because of the vast sums of money involved, most surviving genuine Shakespeare First Folios or Quartos are confined to important museums or libraries, and it is reassuring to know that one of the last major collections in private hands belonged to a bibliophile who had not inherited his money – Paul Francis Webster, who died in America in 1984 at the age of 77. The name probably means little to most of my readers – which is a pity, because Webster was a talented writer whose own 'first edition' works and drafts are already in demand, and may one day be worth considerable sums. Still never heard of him? The reason must be that Webster was a Hollywood song writer, and although the name may not ring a bell even in that context because he was a quiet man who avoided the high profile of some of his contemporaries, he had the talent to win Academy Awards on three occasions: in 1953 for 'Secret Love' from the film *Calamity Jane*; in 1955 with 'Love is a Many-Splendoured Thing' from the film of the same title; and in 1965 with 'The Shadow of your Smile' from *The Sandpiper*.

Song-writing made Webster a rich man, and obviously it takes a fortune to compile books and manuscripts coming into the category of a Shakespeare First Foilo (i.e. the first collected edition of the works, published shortly after his wife's death in 1623), but Webster had an affinity for books as well as words and was very selective; there were only 180 lots in the sale in New York in the year following his death, but each was a gem. The manuscripts ranged from the beautiful, such as a small number of different *Book(s) of Hours,* to dramatically compelling tracts, such as 'Le Combat de la Cordeliere', a 23 leaf poem (with 17 illuminated initials, 2 full page Coats-of-Arms and 2 full page miniatures)[2] on a sea battle between the French and English fleets in 1512. The manuscript was written for Anne of Brittany (1477–1514), Queen of France, but not completed by the time of her death, and finished for her daughter who became Queen of France on the death of her father in 1515.

Among the more modern books in the collection were a copy of *The Posthumous Papers of the Pickwick Club*[3] with an inscription from Dickens to Hans Christian Andersen 'from his friend and admirer', and Flaubert's *Madame Bovary*,[4] one of the most sensational, not to say notorious, novels of the nineteenth century, dedicated to fellow novelist, Champfleury, recognised at the time as leader of the realist school, and who saw the book as a work of genius. In the middle was the First Folio which, in fine condition, fetched $638,000 (the £ at the time equal to £1.22), another indication of Webster's collecting shrewdness because he had purchased it in the 1960s after a New York dealer had picked it up at auction for a mere £23,000. But to me, the most interesting 'association' aspect of this copy, and which I'm sure must have been part of the attraction to the lyricist Webster, is that it had once belonged to the eighteenth century Shakesperian editor, Charles Jennens (1700–73), who was also the librettist for Handel's *Messiah* (there are annotations almost certainly in Jennens' hand).

Returning to the issue of libraries providing a place of concealment for unknown or missing books and manuscripts, the music world was stunned a few years ago when Professor Christopher Wolff studying a collection of organ music by Johann Sebastian Bach in the Reinecke Library at Yale University, came across thirty-three hitherto unknown Bach preludes which had lain undetected since the collection was donated by the American composer Lowell Mason in 1867.

Since Bach's name and reputation have also been taken in vain on a number of occasions, Professor Wolff was faced with a similar problem to Gary Taylor in the Bodleian. The choral preludes, bound in a volume that contained eighty-three works in all, had been entered by a copyist. But a close examination of the music settled any doubts that they had in fact been written by Bach early in his career. Professor Wolff recognised 'innovative tendencies' which could be clearly linked to the composer, and coupled with notations on the score – apart from the provenance – confirmed its authenticity.

Having said that the odds against discovering something very special in an unexpected place were as great as winning the pools, we have to concede that some people were born lucky, but it helps if that person knows something about books or the subject matter. In 1959, a student at University College, Dublin, was browsing through a pile of sixpenny books on a local street barrow when he picked up a copy of *Imaginary Portraits* (1887), by Walter Pater. Inside was stamped 'H.M. Prison Wandsworth', crossed out and replaced by the words 'Reading Prison 272'. To most people it would have meant nothing, but the combination struck a chord, because he had been studying Oscar Wilde who had served two years with hard labour (1895–97) at those prisons for what was then regarded as heinous homosexual offences. It may have been for that reason that Wilde was given a tough time during his spell in confinement, being deprived of what to him must have been basic needs – reading and writing materials. He was forced to write to the Home Secretary to plead in the most humble terms for a relaxation in the terms of his imprisonment . . . for books 'so vital for the preservation of mental balance . . .' that the few books in his possession had been read and re-read until 'they have become almost meaningless'.

The sixpenny Pater was one of those books and pencilled annotations in the margins were probably made by Wilde. Understandably the student hung on to his purchase, although a quarter of a century later, now a senior academic at another university, he put it up for sale at auction where his profit might be said to have been 'substantial'. To the true collector such 'profits' are a bonus, of course, but nothing can compare with the excitement of owning the same book as had been prized in this case, so much by a tragic figure like Oscar Wilde. To the romantic among us, of course, almost every association copy is something to be prized.

Today's more tolerant society has every reason to be embarrassed by the way Oscar Wilde was treated, but in our turn

38

we have little to be smug about; few of us have ever spared a thought for his long suffering wife, Constance, about whom relatively little is known. Yet far from being crushed by the stress of that strange marriage, we now know that in the summer of 1894, when Wilde had gone off with Lord Alfred Douglas, she actually had an affair with the then manager and senior partner of the still thriving Hatchard's bookshop in London's Piccadilly (the fact that she frequented any bookshop automatically elevates Constance in my esteem!) The relationship remained a secret outside the immediate family of the young man, Arthur Lee Humphreys, for almost a hundred years (and certainly not appreciated by her two biographers) until two of her letters[5] to him (one of 8 pages, the other of 4) turned up at auction.

Constance Wilde was thirty-six at the time, and Humphreys seven years her junior, and the shorter of the letters written just before her husband's trial when her morale must have been at its lowest, leaves little doubt of her feelings: 'I *have* been happy, and I *do* love you dear Arthur. Nothing in my life has ever made me so happy as this love of yours to me has done . . . I love you just because you ARE, and because you have come into my life to fill it with love and make it rich . . .' Humphreys, despite his relative youth, was presumably a man of some intellect, being an author and publisher as well as bookseller, and although their friendship was known and accepted no one (apart, possibly, from Oscar Wilde) suspected it was of an intimate nature. Nor does it appear to have been a case of infatuation, because the same letter went on to confess that she loved him also for being 'dear to the children, and nice to Oscar too . . .'

Most reputable booksellers operate on the principle that it is immoral not to pay a fair price when buying from an unsuspecting member of the public, but that other booksellers and people in the trade are fair game since they should know what they are doing – as indeed, they should. However, the specialist in modern first editions cannot be expected to be an authority on incunabula, and with very old books the problem is accentuated as soon as we move away from literature or history. The most remarkable 'bargain' in many years was picked up at a little known auction on the Isle of Wight in 1986 by one dealer who was more knowledgeable than the others in attendance when it came to identifying what the catalogue described as a box of old documents. He recognised the author of the collection of letters and working drafts as Thomas Malthus (1766–1834), the political economist, whose highly respected works include *Essay on the Principle of Population as it affects the Future Improvement of Society, 1798,* which inspired Charles Darwin to develop his theory of 'natural selection'. Unable to prove his suspicion on the spot, but confident that anything from the pen of Malthus was very special, he telephoned the old established London booksellers, Maggs Brothers, to ask if they would back his judgement if the bidding proved to be beyond his own budget. They did, and the lot was knocked down for £2,000. It was only after closer examination in London that the true importance of the documents was appreciated and the Malthus papers were subsequently sold to an agent representing 'international interests' for a figure believed to be approaching £400,000!

Even the most experienced auction houses make mistakes, which – when one considers the breadth of their coverage – is only to be expected, provided that it is only once in a while. A typical example was in 1986 when a leading London firm was offering an exceptionally scarce magazine, *Aurora Australis,* printed and published in 1908 at the winter headquarters of Sir Ernest Shackleton's British Antarctic Expedition. The catalogue pointed out that only one hundred copies had been printed and the copy on offer had the original board covers made from the expedition's packing cases. It contained eleven lithographs of etchings by George Marston, the party's resident artist, a preface by Shackleton in his capacity as editor-in-chief, and articles by members of the party. The unusual printer's credit read: 'Printed at the Sign of the Penguins by Joyce and Wild*. Latitude 77° . . . 32' South; Longtitude 166° . . . 12' East. Antarctica.'

Had I been at the sale I would not have doubted the auctioneer's estimate of £500–£600, but then my knowledge of polar material is superficial. Someone in a better position to judge was Dr D. W. H. Walton, of Bluntisham Books, specialists in this area, and who had recently reprinted the classic. In writing subsequently to *The*

**Members of the team who had been given a cursory knowledge of typesetting and printing by the manufacturers of the printing press which had been presented to the expedition.*

Bookdealer, he pointed out not only the undervaluation, but further reasons for the magazine's rarity – that there is no clear evidence that a hundred copies were ever printed; a worldwide survey over five years identified less than sixty copies, although it was possible that a greater number were printed of one or two of the individual contributions. He also revealed that many of the original copies are partly defective due to problems with collating a book of single leaves with no page numbers. However, fortunately for the vendor, there were a few dealers at the sale who recognised the magazine for what it is.[6]

But even when the auction house is correct in its estimate and in fixing the reserve price, the lot does not necessarily sell. To me, the greatest surprise in recent years was the apparent lack of interest shown in the private diary of Captain Lewis Edward Nolan the officer who carried the order which led to the destruction of the heroic Light Brigade by the Russian artillery in the Crimea in 1854 – the most romanticised cavalry charge in British military history, and which inspired Tennyson's epic poem:

> Theirs not to reason why
> Theirs but to do and die;
> Into the valley of Death
> Rode the six hundred . . .

Show me the Englishman who is not moved by the disastrous Charge of the Light Brigade, whether inspired by Cecil Woodham-Smith's gripping story *The Reason Why*; the ridiculously confused but exciting Hollywood account with Errol Flynn playing Nolan, or the more responsible later British film with David Hemmings as Nolan. The only drawback to an enthralling diary covering the period 5 September to 12 October (the first five weeks of the campaign) is that it ends a couple of weeks before Nolan's death in the charge, and thus throws no new light on the mystery surrounding his interpretation of the order given to him by Lord Raglan (he was the Commander's express choice because of his skill as a rider) for Lord Lucan to attack; however, it adds considerably to what was already known of him as a dedicated soldier as opposed to the romantic hero image.

Apart from his prowess as a cavalry officer, Nolan would have made an excellent war reporter; his descriptive powers harnessed to a comprehensive grasp of military tactics. (His *Cavalry: its history and tactics* appeared in 1853, followed by a French translation in Paris the following year, and his *Training of Cavalry Remount Horses*, was published posthumously in 1861.) The journal, written in a commercial notebook, consisted of ninety-seven pages and had seven neatly drawn sketch maps or orders of march, one coloured. Typical of his detailed account of the war was this extract from a description of the Battle of Alma, illustrated with a map.

'The Russians had marked their ranges with white willow wands, thus almost every shot from their heavy guns told. I saw one myself when walking back, carrying my saddle after my horse had been killed. I saw the round shot strike several times into the ranks of the 30th Regt. which was lying down under fire, and as I came up towards them the men several times called to me "Look out sir, there it comes on your right or your left . . ."

. . . In passing through the vineyards under a fearful fire the men slung their muskets and picked grapes, betting with each other who shd. have time left to finish his bunch before being bowled over.'

His anecdotes enliven the stuff of mere military history. '. . . Sir George Brown going round his outposts got in front of the chain of sentries, who taking for granted must be an enemy as he appeared to be coming from Sebastopol, they at once opened fire upon him. "What did you do, Sir George, did you lie down?"

"Lie down, no. I stood still and swore at them." '

The bidding for this important journal reached £8,000 and petered out . . . incredible.

A book which is anything but 'perfect' in the aesthetic sense – yet is treasured for its historical novelty, and its significance in the seventeenth and eighteenth centuries when a growing proportion of the population was beginning to read – is the chap-book, an early form of paperback.

Because they were poorly produced, of paper covers; indifferently printed and with woodcut illustrations somewhat distorted, relatively few have survived considering the large numbers published – hence part of the attraction to collectors. The name derives from chapmen, itinerant travelling salesmen – often depicted carrying a tray of cheap novelties – peddling their wares from town to village; the lurid chap-books designed for adults and children – being the TV of the day. Although they are associated mainly with the eighteenth century, their history is much older; there are references to chapmen in Shakespeare's plays. It is known that they were popular in France in that century, probably before catching on in England, but eventually most of the popular books of the day (i.e. *Robinson Crusoe*), were being printed in this form, greatly cut to accommodate the format.

Despite the low production standards, it should not be assumed that they did not have their merits. They appealed to a wide audience, and even educated people – especially in the children's format. Johnson's biographer James Boswell, writes in *Boswell's London*, how in 1763 at the age of twenty-two, he still had nostalgic memories.

> . . . Some days ago I went to the old printing-office in Bow Churchyard kept by Dicey, whose family have kept it fourscore years. There are ushered into the world of literature, Jack & the Giants, the Seven Wise Men of Gotham, and other story books which in my dawning years amused me as much as *Rasselas* does now. I saw the whole scheme with a kind of pleasing romantic feeling to find myself where all the old darlings were printed. I bought two dozen books and had them bound up with this title, *Curious Productions* . . . [Dicey was a publisher of chap-books for what was known as the 'running' stationery trade.]

They remained popular until the middle of the nineteenth century when the sector of the market for which they catered was weaned away to the 'new' vogue in periodicals, which were able to offer a much higher standard, and original material.

One of the biggest collections of children's chap-books in private hands belonged to the authors of so many books on children's literature, Peter and Iona Opie; it subsequently went to the Bodleian Library, which already had a substantial collection, probably second only to that at Harvard.

The value of pre-publication material is obvious, especially when it deals with ideas or events of special significance, but today the broad rule of thumb lesson is not to throw *anything* away – and if you are lucky enough to be on hand at some great event it might even be worth going through the wastepaper bins. One of the most surprising items on offer at the Barry R. Levin Science Fiction and Fantasy auction (see Chapter 3) was a *press release*! Admittedly it dealt with an historic occasion – man's first walk on the moon – but it was merely a report hastily prepared by America's Space Agency for the world's press in attendance, and once used, consigned to the waste bin. The catalogue entry read:

Armstrong (Neil), APPOLLO II MISSION COMMENTARY 7–20–69 CDT 20:30 GET 108: 02 330/2 First printed announcement of man's first steps on the moon & of the first words spoken while standing on its surface. 26 sheets, single staple, laid in loose in cloth portfolio. (Houston: Mission Control, 1969)

This historic document was issued by Mission Control about ten minutes after Armstrong first stepped onto the surface of the Moon.

It is a verbatim report of the words spoken between Mission Control and Armstrong and contains the now famous first words spoken by man from the surface of the Moon. 'That's one small step for man. One giant leap for mankind.' Armstrong won a special Hugo Award for 'the best Moon landing ever'.

The man who 'saved' the report from destruction happened to be a Texan bookseller, fortunate enough to be invited to the ceremony. What had been given away free fetched $425 at the sale.

Interesting, sometimes valuable material will always be lost or destroyed through ignorance, either without a second's thought, or for what are considered at the time good 'practical' reasons. It was not uncommon, for example, for bookbinders over the centuries to use paper and vellum from older books to 'build-up' covers between leather and boards, in some cases to produce something that in terms of history or scholarship was inferior to the original (see Chapter 7). It was particularly rampant in the sixteenth century when many literary treasures in the form of vellum manuscripts from the monasteries suppressed by Henry VIII had only one value – as scrap! Such outrages included the use of two leaves of a thirteenth-century manuscript containing a life of St. Modwenna (an Irish princess baptised by St. Patrick) by Geoffrey Abbot of Burton-on-Trent from 1114–50, as a rough cover for a reference book of 1550, containing Acts of Parliament.

The most recent example was the discovery in 1986 of a 2ft × 9 inch vellum fragment of what is thought to be the first English 'modern' world map – and it comprised the binding for a fifteenth-century estate rent book. Complete medieval wall maps have virtually disappeared (the only known surviving thirteenth century example is at Hereford Cathedral), and even fragments are extremely rare, the last significant 'find' being in Germany in 1911. The book, containing records of the lands of Walter Aslake at Creake Abbey in Norfolk, was compiled in 1483–4, and as such has an interest in its own right, although in no way unique. It was housed for many generations in a tin trunk at the home of a Barnet housewife who, unable to comprehend binding or contents, took it to the British Library for an opinion.

Because of the age of the vellum binding, and the way it had been kept, it was difficult to see much with the naked eye, but under ultraviolet light, experts were able to identify the map, drawn between 1325–75. Apart from its rarity, the importance of the fragment is that it indicates that modern sea charts reached England much earlier than previously believed, and it is possible to speculate that such an advanced knowledge of the shape of the world may well have contributed to England's commercial and military success at the time. It also challenges the previously accepted supremacy of Germany and Italy in medieval cartography.

In view of its shape and the figures shown, to the uninitiated the Aslake map (as it is now called) looks more Egyptian than English. This is probably because medieval wall maps were orientated differently, with the East at the top and, from 1110, Jerusalem at the centre. The world is shown as a disc surrounded by islands with fabulous creatures (depicted from about 1200) at the fringe. The fragment shows the Red Sea, Africa and the Atlantic islands, and an unidentified part of Europe. Identification was made easier by the remarkable coincidence of a discovery a year earlier of a fragment, thought to date between 1220–50, also showing part of Africa. The property of the Duchy of Cornwall, it had also been used as the cover for a court book for the manor of Hemel Hempstead, and since the last entry was 1523, it is probable that was also the date of binding.

The circumstances of the map fragment's incorporation into the rent book are intriguing. Large wall maps were often used as a backcloth for altars, and although Walter Aslake lived at Creake Abbey it was also large enough to accommodate a small group of Augustinian monks. For reasons not known, the abbey was destroyed by arson some time before February 1484, and the map was almost certainly damaged. Aslake helped rebuild the abbey, but because of the coincidence of the dates of the fire and entries in the book, it is reasonable to suppose the remains of the map were cut up and used as binding materials.

But that theory opens another dramatic line of further investigation. When the monks died from the Black Death plague in 1506 the books were bequeathed to the University of Cambridge, which suggests that other estate books bound in that period may also have incorporated fragments of the map. Subsequently the British Library entered into negotiations with the librarian at Christ's College, Cambridge, to see if it was possible to investigate without damaging the books involved; although photographs would probably be sufficient – eliminating an interesting conservation problem. It reminds me of a delightful bookshop in North Wales, the Old Court House at Caerwys run by Tom Lloyd-Roberts, which has a long and fascinating history (the house has its origins in the fifteenth century, although a plain stone wall at the rear is believed to be part of the court of Prince David, last of the Welsh princes, two centuries earlier). The irony is that the front of the house, redecorated in 1800, is a particularly attractive example of Georgian style which merits the Preservation Order placed on it; but when Tom Lloyd-Roberts began to find interesting Tudor features beneath, he was prevented by that order from investigating further.

But talking of conservation, a subject dealt with in greater length elsewhere, the British Library, intent on putting the Aslake fragment (which they had purchased) and the other on loan from the Duchy of Cornwall (the Prince of Wales) on display as major parts of a 'Lost Worlds' exhibition of manuscripts, had to tackle the problem from the outset. When it was brought in, it was tightly rolled, badly infected by mould and extremely fragile, though the red lettering of the map could be seen. Stage one was to fumigate it to get rid of the live mould, and then 'relax' the vellum by exposure to moisture in a carefully controlled manner over a number of days; only then could it be safely opened. The thong that attached the map to the rental was removed so that the map could be seen as a whole, and only at this point was it realised that the thong was another fragment of the map!

Although we have our individual preferences, it cannot be disputed that in general terms, early manuscripts have a fascination that is unique. Not only were they produced in more violent times – death and destruction decimating the numbers surviving the centuries – but many were one-off works of art; even when copies were made, each was individually crafted, and different to the next. Some were so magnificent that at auction they have been categorised as works of art, and one masterpiece, a twelfth-century manuscript, *The Gospels of Henry the Lion*, sold at Sotheby's in 1983 for £7.4M not only broke the auction record for a book (£1.05M for the Gutenberg Bible in 1978) but at that time even for a work of art (£6.4M for 'Juliet and her Nurse' by Turner in 1980).

The final bid by the international 'team' of booksellers, Bernard Quaritch and Hans P. Kraus, representing a West German consortium, staggered the book world (Sotheby's who recognised its potential interest estimated a sale price of between £2–£4M), yet it was later revealed that the buyers considered they had gained a bargain, and if necessary would have gone to £10M! So, what could have been so special about yet another beautiful medieval manuscript?

Well, the West German Government, which had provided the bulk of the money together with two of the State Governments and private donations, had no doubts. They described their purchase as 'one of the most important and precious art treasures of German culture', and that German culture and history were 'uniquely manifested' in the manuscript. Sotheby's head of Western Illuminated Manuscripts department, Dr Christopher de Hamel, who researched and identified the long lost *Gospel*, described it as the most important manuscript of its kind to come on to the open market this century, and the greatest still in private hands. Although essentially German it contains the only contemporary portrait of Henry II of England, and the earliest surviving picture of St. Thomas à Becket.

47

Henry the Lion (c.1129–95), is as legendary a figure in German history as Richard the Lionheart of England. Conqueror and crusader, he was the founder of Munich and owner of vast estates in Scandinavia, Austria, and Lombardy, as well as Germany where he was Duke of Saxony, Count of Brunswick and Duke of Bavaria. In 1168 he married Matilda, daughter of Henry II of England, and thus sister of the above Richard, and the infamous King John. Despite his enormous power, he fell from grace and was subsequently exiled to his father-in-law's court in England. Meanwhile, Henry had commissioned the manuscript, measuring 13½ inches by 10 inches and consisting of 226 leaves with 41 sumptuous full-page illuminations, from a Benedictine monk, for presentation to Brunswick Cathedral. The present binding dates from the sixteenth century, but because the book does not appear to have been opened very much or exposed to light, the condition of the contents is remarkably fine and bright.

The manuscript is presumed to have been taken from Brunswick Cathedral by the Emperor Charles IV and installed in Prague Cathedral some time in the following century. It was then purchased by the King of Hanover in the 1860s, and taken to Schloss Cumberland at Gmunden in Austria when the Hanoverian dynasty was exiled by Bismarck. It was removed by its owners, descendants of the Dukes of Brunswick, in the late 1930s and changed hands privately after World War II, since when it had been kept outside Germany, remaining unseen until the auction.

There is a direct link between the *Gospel of Henry the Lion* and four pages of an illuminated manuscript appertaining to the life of St. Thomas à Becket, which turned up at Sotheby's three years later to set another kind of record when it was won by J. Paul Getty for £1.4M, or as our grocery-list inspired collectors would calculate – £350,000 per page!

The assassination of Becket in Canterbury Cathedral in 1170 was one of the landmarks in the early struggle between monarchy and church in England, and the Becket Leaves, as they have become known, deals with the relationship between the Archbishop and Henry II. The two men were featured so graphically in the illuminations for the *Gospel* because, presumably for family reasons, Henry sided with his father-in-law against Becket and the Pope (Alexander III). The leaves (because of their historical

48

significance, they were later displayed at the British Library) had come from a private collection in Belgium to where they can be traced at the time of the French Revolution. Nothing is known of their earlier history, but it is reasonable to suppose that anything sympathetic to Becket would have been suppressed by successive English kings, and probably taken to the Continent. At one stage they too had been used as 'padding' for a binding.

So blasé have we become that European material surviving from the twelfth century is taken for granted; its value generally depending on the quality of the illumination, but even scholars were awed when a manuscript (two leaves of vellum), believed to be the earliest known piece of English handwriting of any kind, turned up in 1984; it dates from the *seventh* century! Since it is known that the Venerable Bede possessed a copy of the same text from which he often quoted, and which was a considerable influence on his own *Ecclesiastical History of the English People* a hundred years later, it is possible to speculate that it may even have been the same copy.

Two other fascinating features of the manuscript[7] are (a) that it turned up in a library – the excellent Folger Shakespeare Library, in Washington DC – where it had 'disappeared' for almost fifty years. In the library's defence it should be remembered that because of its specialist nature, staff and readers would not expect to encounter a medieval manuscript which explains why (b) it was found in a box containing a Renaissance printed book *of which it formed the binding* – although, as we have seen, that was a far more common practice than anyone might have imagined.

The existence of the manuscript (a double-page fragment known as a bifolium) was previously unknown. Two hundred years older than the famous *Book of Kells* (although that is a huge work in four volumes), it was written on both sides in Irish half-uncial script by a monk, probably in a Northumbrian monastery. Sotheby's also claimed that it was the earliest Anglo-Irish manuscript to come on to the market (for obvious reasons, the Folger Library decided to sell) since the Vikings raided Jarrow in 1022, stealing the monastery's art treasures. The text is a Latin translation by Rufinus of *Historia Ecclesiastica* by Eusebius (AD 265–340), Bishop of Caesarea (Palestine).

Thirteen hundred years were to elapse before the introduction of the Penguin paperback which, although not by any means a new concept, revolutionised reading habits in the United Kingdom. This may seem a far cry from the perfect or ideal book, but some people are far more interested in early Penguins than rare manuscripts. In 1985, Phillips the London auction house celebrated the imprint's 50th anniversary with a sale of over 3,000 first editions – partly a commercial undertaking, the rest of the proceeds (in the main copies owned and signed by their authors) going to book-related charities.

Because the auction was breaking new ground there could be no precedent for the prices obtained, but among the more interesting lots (and apart from non-paperback material also donated by some authors) were: a first edition of the first Penguin, *Ariel*,[8] by Andre Maurois (estimated price £30); a proof copy of D. H. Lawrence's *Lady Chatterley's Lover*,[9] printed by Hazell, Watson & Viney, who withdrew from printing before the trial! (est. £10–£15); a signed and limited to 500 copies edition of *May We Borrow Your Husband*),[10] by Graham Greene (est. £40–£50).

The gathering of so many Penguin collectors prompted Phillips to reveal the anecdote of the collector who had the first 1,500 except one, for which he hunted for many years – until Penguin pointed out that for some peculiar reason that number had never been issued!

To many collectors, the most compelling items of all are autographed letters and diaries, but in the past few years interest has jumped from levels that had always been steady to what now can only be described as hysterical. Much of the 'sudden' clamour has developed with the growing awareness of the significant gaps in our knowledge of social history, e.g. the rise of movements such as Civil Rights, or CND. In 1986 I thought prices had reached a peak when an American collector at Christie's in New York, paid £151,724 for a letter from Albert Einstein to President F. D. Roosevelt, which hastened the building of an atomic bomb. One appreciates that a letter by definition is unique and this, known as the letter that started it all, must have been one of the most important documents of the twentieth century – but that is still a lot of money. However, jaws really dropped towards the end of that year, when a world record was established at Sotheby's, New York, for a letter from Thomas Jefferson (admittedly of special significance because of its strong attack on anti-Semitism), knocked down to the Yeshira University Museum, New York, for – \$396,000! (= £269,387: estimated price was £15,000–£25,000).

Some semblance of sanity was restored at the subsequent sale in London of a whole archive of unpublished letters[11] from Mahatma Gandhi to a white South African disciple – over 250 spanning the eventful period between 1909 and 1946. The most important Gandhi collection ever offered at auction, they were written to Hermann Kallenbach from a variety of places, from a Pretoria gaol; Tolstoy Farm (the commune in South Africa for which Kallenbach gave him the land); an Aliens Detention camp in India; and cover the spectrum of religious, philosophical and political thinking. Rightly the letters were purchased by the Indian Government.

Strange how interest in Gandhi has fluctuated over the years. Until the epic film, he was very much a distant and eccentric figure to all but the politically aware. In 1948, a small English publishing firm, Phoenix House, managed to get the English rights for publication in the West of the great man's autobiography written in the late 1920s (and which had obviously sold exceptionally well in India). They printed a very modest 7,000 copies, and had reason to feel elated by the reviews, yet sales were so disappointing that by the end of 1949 the book, published at 21s (£1.05) was remaindered at one shilling (5 pence)!

Having been a bibliophile for most of my life, I still get a little confused at times in defining the parameters of collecting. I suppose, for example, that one of the answers to the riddle: 'when is a book not a book?' is – 'when it's a work of art' – such as the *Gospels of Henry the Lion*. Yet that was sold as a book, and one can appreciate why. But take as another example, modern binding. There is no question that some of the more 'ambitious' bindings today are intended as art objects, and if the owner wanted to read the contents he would obtain a paperback copy. Some of these bindings are magnificent (and often need to be for their cost), but the surprise to me is that, with few exceptions, they are bought by book and not art collectors. They are reviewed or evaluated in art/craft terms, yet displayed by their owners – individuals or libraries and museums, in the context of the history of book production.

Music is another case in point. If we found an unknown music score manuscript or a cache of correspondence between famous composers we would take it/them to a bookseller, not a music shop, because the potential sale would be to bibliophiles or libraries. Original scores from the great composers turn up often enough at auction to get some idea of the high prices that might be realised. I look forward with interest to a thesis one of these days on the status of composers in collecting terms. '. . . Beethoven's symphonies were overrated, but his "first editions" are excellent value . . .'

In the interim, some of the auction room performances have been quite spectacular, with prices usually reflecting the same criteria as book manuscripts – rarity. In recent years some of the most interesting lots appearing at Sotheby's London auditorium have been: a lost Overture to the opera *Fierabras* by Schubert (1797–1828)[12]; Wagner's autographed manuscript of the Overtures to *Tannhaüser*, described as one of the finest in private hands; and an autographed manuscript of part of Chopin's *Variations on Mozart's 'La ci darem la Mano'*.

The Schubert Overture written in 1823 was the most substantial, and most poignant; a full-score running to sixty pages in his own hand, it bears annotations that suggest he was planning a performance, although sadly this did not take place until 1829, a year after his early death. After being lost for many years, its reappearance was regarded as a major discovery for music scholarship. The estimated price was £150,000–£200,000.

Wagner's Overture manuscript, signed and dated by him in Dresden in 1845, was expected to fetch a similar figure. Now one of his most popular works, it was first conducted in a concert hall by Mendelssohn, although his performance was described by Wagner's father-in-law, the conductor Hans von Bülow, as 'an execution, not only in the figurative, but also in the literal sense of the term.' It should be borne in mind that the value of original manuscripts such as this is not merely one of historical nostalgia but in the light they throw on the composer's thinking. In this case, for example, there are a number of differences from the first printing; the last chord is three bars longer than in the orchestral version, which indicates that at a later stage Wagner (1813–83) incorporated a few refinements. Earlier in that month two of his minor works were sold – the first an early draft of three songs he wrote in Paris (£12,100), and a complete manuscript of *Götterdämmerung*, written out for him but probably corrected by the composer (£8,250). However, all these figures were dwarfed by Wagner's handwritten manuscript of the libretto of *Lohengrin* which fetched £187,000, something book collectors can appreciate a little more than a series of black dots and strange markings laid out at apparent random across a music score.

The Chopin variations, written in 1827 when he was only 17, and based on the theme from Mozart's *Don Giovanni*, was the composition which inspired his contemporary, Schumann to salute him with the now famous words: 'Hat's off, Gentlemen – A genius!' That was four years later, but Schumann's admiration took a practical form, because he persuaded his future wife, Clara Wieck, to give the music its first public airing in Leipzig. Manuscripts handwritten by Chopin are extremely rare, and although this was only two pages, it was expected to fetch between £40,000–£60,000.

In another case – of four choral works by Handel (1685–1759) – the music, if slightly less distinguished, came to light in more interesting circumstances. Found in a Manchester toy cupboard they had, in fact, passed through the same auction room in 1879 when they were unrecognised and sold, according to the catalogue as 'Various compositions for organ and voices . . . probably all unpublished . . . a parcel.' Now they were identified as the original instrumental and vocal parts of four sacred works, belonging to his 'Carmelite Music' series, composed when the young Handel was in Rome in 1707. Sotheby's were able to trace the history of the manuscripts in the two hundred years since their disappearance from Rome.

The works were orginally commissioned by Cardinal Carlo Colonna and the manuscripts remained in the Colonna library until the mid-nineteenth century when it was broken up and sold. The Handel works were bought by an English clergyman, and when he died no one knew the provenance – they had been written out by copyists, and the scribbled annotations by the composer were not recognised. The successful bidder for the anonymous parcel was a collector of music who subsequently presented them to a singer, Eva Nellie Brown, who in turn gave them to her son when he was learning the piano. That is how they ended up in the toy cupboard until many years later when his wife decided to take a look. This time they were identified and eventually sold for £88,000.

There are comparable cases, but I would like to leave the music world with a glimpse of the composer, not so much a symbol of greatness, but as an individual with ordinary human frailties. The arts in the nineteenth century have acquired a romantic image, no doubt because so many young men and women touched with genius died in tragic circumstances, or were afflicted by illness and physical handicaps in some especially cruel way. Composers are well represented, and Beethoven immediately springs to mind; deafness surely being the most terrible blow.

It is a widely held belief that artists and musicians *need* to suffer to give full expression to their genius; but saying that men like Beethoven only lived for their music, is as trite as suggesting that nurses are so dedicated to healing the sick they are not concerned with being adequately paid. Dedication deserves some form of recompense as well as the satisfaction of creating beautiful music, or art, or doing a job well. Beethoven never married, but in his letters and diaries he makes reference to having loved only one woman – someone he could not have. On his death, among his papers was found an unsent letter to the woman who has become known as his 'Immortal Beloved', although there was no name by which she might be identified at the time.

However, detective work by Maynard Solomon, author of a biography published in 1980, identifies her as Antonie von Brentano, ten years his junior, who had then been married to a man she admired but not loved for fourteen years (since she was 18). In 1985 a letter[13] from Beethoven to Antonie thought to have been lost was sold (it was dated February 1816 – an estimated four years after the more passionate unsent message), together with an engraved portrait of himself which, the letter states, revealed his soul. Although he also addresses his sentiments to her husband and her children, he says to her: '. . . But to you I send my best greetings and merely add that I gladly recall to mind the hours which I have spent . . . hours which to me are the most unforgettable . . .'

Beethoven dedicated his *Thirty-Three Variations on a Waltz by Diabelli* (Opus 120) to her in 1823, and his song *An die Geliebte* ('To the Beloved'), written in 1812, is known to have been given to her.

At least Schumann's love for Clara Wieck, daughter of his teacher who opposed their match for three years, ended happily. And evidence survives of their relationship in the form of two contrasting types of communication which appeared at auction almost 150 years later. The first was written in 1837, when Clara was only eighteen and forbidden to see her lover; a scribbled note attempting to arrange a secret meeting when her father would be away in Prague for a couple of days. The other was a three page, forty-line poem written by the composer in 1840, after her father had relented and allowed them to marry:

> Egmonts Geliebte Klärchen hiess –
> O Name wundersuss!
>
> Lorbeeren der kunstlerin
> Nicht übel stehn –
> Myrthe vom Mädchen
> Ueber alles schön
>
> Ich habe eine gute Braut –
> We sie geschaut,
> Auf Weibertreu baut . . .

Schumann's love for his wife, manifested in the form of a number of songs and chamber works, was to remain constant, and another sale, a piano composition for her fortieth birthday fetched £15,400.

One of the most broadly interesting collections of papers to come up for auction in recent years, were those of John Montagu, 4th Earl of Sandwich, relating to his sponsorship as First Lord of the Admiralty, of the explorer, Captain James Cook (1728–79). They contain all the elements of adventure, throwing light on a range of subjects, from academic to sociological – man's fortitude, and human relations. Cook was one of the greatest explorers. Remembered principally for his charting of New Zealand, the east coast of Australia, and the discovery of a large number of tropical islands, the extent of his travels is not generally appreciated; as far north as North America and Canada in his early days, to parts of Antarctica. Shortly before his death, his latest discovery had been what he was to name in honour of his sponsor, the Sandwich Islands, to which he returned – driven back to shelter from bad weather conditions. This time he was murdered by natives on Hawaii in a dispute that in retrospect seems so unnecessary.

The collection is made up mainly of correspondence, including letters from Cook; Joseph Banks, the naturalist, who had accompanied Cook some of the time; Captain Charles Clerke, who had been with Cook on all three expeditions and who was to take command after his death (Clerke, in his ship *Discovery*, was late in his final rendezvous with Cook's *Resolution*, a delay explained by his letter to Sandwich – from prison, where he had been held for his brother's debts!); and King George III, one paying tribute to his explorer.

Perhaps the most dramatic was Cook's last letter[14] to Sandwich from the Cape of Good Hope, written in November 1776 before setting off on the last lap of his ill-fated third voyage. It arrived in England five months later, and although he was to write several other letters they did not arrive until after his death. In it he reports having added considerably to the numbers of animals on board (food and provisions were expected to last two years and upwards), and 'Nothing is wanting but a few females of our own species to make the Resolution a Compleate Arke . . .'

In another letter, he thanks his sponsor for 'the many favors conferred upon me, and in particular for the Very liberal allowance made to Mrs Cook during my absence. This, by enabling my family to live at ease and removing from them every fear of indigency, has set my heart at rest and filled it with gratitude to my Noble benefactor . . .' The captain's journals were published in 1784 and Elizabeth Cook, who was to survive him for fifty-six years, was granted half the profits, amounting to over £2,000, a considerable sum in those days.

But enough of this solemnity. Letters do not have to make any contribution to history to be collectable; indeed, the frivolous have an appeal of their own – such as one from Dorothy L. Sayers, describing her search for the ideal actor to play the part of her creation, Lord Peter Wimsey: '. . . my dear, my heart is BROKEN! I have seen the *perfect* Peter Wimsey. Height, voice, charm, smile, manner, outline of features, *everything* – and he is – THE CHAPLAIN OF BALLIOL!'

Inevitably, with any personal selection, there are bound to be gaps, and I am conscious of having omitted a couple of categories important to some – especially one: natural history colour plate books, which are among the most costly and sought after; indeed, J. J. Audubon's four volume *Birds of America* (1827–38) is probably the most expensive of all 'modern' books. Yet while I can appreciate the magnificence of Audubon's drawings (there are 435 plates, 1065 figures), or those of his British equivalent, John Gould, they might just as well be sold as paintings – which is frequently what happens with 'breakers', battered copies broken up for their plates. They say that beauty is only skin deep and, in my opinion, that is especially true of this type of book; I believe books should have an appeal beyond their appearance. Admittedly, original Audubon material is thin on the ground, which means that one is also paying for rarity, but if I had a million pounds to spare I wouldn't have much difficulty in finding a whole selection of choice items. Equally, a hundred collectors given the same funds would no doubt find a hundred different permutations – thank goodness.

Auction Prices Attained (including Buyer's Premium)

1.	'Shakespeare' notebook	£165,000	(£ = $1.51)
2.	Le Combat	$16,500	(£ = $1.22)
3.	Dickens	$22,000	(ditto)
4.	Flaubert	$8,250	(ditto)
5.	Constance Wilde letters	£2,750 each	(£ = $1.48)
6.	*Aurora Australia*	£7,500	(£ = $1.42)
7.	7th century manuscript	£82,000	(£ = $1.35)
8.	*Ariel*	£120	(£ = $1.49)
9.	Lawrence	£120	(ditto)
10.	Greene	£90	(ditto)
11.	Gandhi letters	£154,000	(£ = $1.51)
12.	Schubert manuscript	£165,000	(£ = $1.58)
13.	Beethoven manuscript	£55,000	(£ = $1.29)
14.	Captain Cook letter	£16,500	(£ = $1.48)

Three

INVESTMENT: HOT BOOKS OR HOT AIR?

Human nature being what it is, people hanker for the 'good old days'. By 'good', they invariably mean when everything was cheaper, conveniently forgetting the less attractive features of the past – even if it were true that price rises have been consistent. Relating book prices to income, there have been periods when the collector has had good reason for complaint; others when books – new and secondhand – have been cheap. But price fluctuations apart, book collecting has not changed much over the centuries. In the beginning, perhaps, there was little effort involved; usually a matter of being prepared to take what was on offer. As desirable books became less accessible, and the bibliophile began to acquire the knowledge necessary to hunt down his quarry, so colllecting took on another dimension – it is, after all, the fun of the chase that makes any acquisition so rewarding.

So, as collectors sought to share their good fortune, to demonstrate to the unenlightened the pervading satisfaction to be derived from books, interest snowballed, and with it the elements of greater competition. The first to be assimilated were largely scholars involved in literature, history and politics, but eventually they were joined by others who, in some cases, had never read a book for choice – soldiers or sportsmen interested in books on warfare or cricket; by railway or motor enthusiasts; by men and women interested in magic, dolls, card games, or travel. It was a natural progression to be welcomed.

The bee crash-landed in the honey about twenty-five years ago, when a few innovative booksellers began to promote the concept of books as an investment; to lecture business groups on the viability of books as an alternative to stocks and shares. For the first time people began to regard books as commodities, totally unconcerned with what was printed between the covers. In much the same way that architects in every century come up with 'new' theories of design, e.g. 'high rise' flats, without thought for social consequences, so these enterprising booksellers intent on developing new markets, failed to anticipate the possible drawbacks. The person who has not only never read a book for choice, but who does not even care what he/she collects if it can be regarded as an investment, may in due course, distort market values – not so very different to the way in the mid-1980s the American stock market was thrown into confusion by a spate of company take-overs financed by sharp dealers after a quick cut-and-run profit.

To condemn the philosophy of books as an investment is over-simplifying the issue. It is, after all, an indisputable fact that a rare volume of special merit in one sense or another can only appreciate in value – the bottom is never going to fall out of the Gutenberg Bible market – but the person who can afford to buy on a grand scale has a wide choice of alternative investments available. The investment lobby going for the middle ground – to people who might have some spare funds not already invested – promoted a message that attracted people for the wrong reasons. Indeed, so seductive is the apparently innocent theme 'collecting for fun and profit', that most of us welcomed the influx as though demand could only stimulate trade. It did, to such an extent that new book-collecting journals were launched to cash-in on the bigger audience; but the demand thus created may yet turn out to be an illusion. As I said in the introduction, the serious discussion of prices relating to ordinary or commonplace books, is reducing the excitement of book collecting to the level of buying groceries.

Despite the number of arguments in favour of or against books as an investment, the genuine collector will confirm the old adage that the only motivation should be the desire to collect what appeals to us in its own right; that way it does not matter whether values go up or down. Nor do our purchases need to be rationalised. As R. M. Williamson pointed out in his *Bits From an Old Bookshop*, more than eighty years ago: 'During the early phase of the disease, the book-lover is content to purchase only books which he reads. Next he buys books which he means to read: and as his store accumulates, he hopes to read his purchases; but by-and-by he takes home books in beautiful bindings and of early date, but printed in extinct languages he cannot read.'

Of course, the bibliophile hopes that his collecting activities may also show a substantial profit on his transactions – if only as a 'property' to be inherited by his dependants – but only from buying by instinct or inclination can one get complete satisfaction (Samuel Johnson said much the same about reading) and develop the knowledge necessary to increase one's awareness and confidence. Unless he really knows his subject the ordinary collector can easily come unstuck if buying purely for investment. I say 'ordinary' because the rich person can dabble in the most expensive books which have a steadily appreciating value which is not likely to be affected by the fashions that influence prices in most other sectors. The return on that investment is another matter.

For those who disagree, I offer the following evidence. The only time the premise has actually been put to the test was in England about six years ago, although the programme ended prematurely. The investment portfolio was the brain-child of old-established and respected London antiquarian booksellers, Francis Edwards, and directed at people who were not in the habit of buying books. Supported by impressive figures from *The Economist* Intelligence Unit report showing that rare books (along with paintings) topped the investment performance table for arts and antiques, Francis Edwards went to the City with an offer to package a number of books representing a cross-section of interest, for a minimum investment of £500. The trade was horrified.

The concept was so startling that in 1981 I wrote an article 'Laying Down Rare Books' for *The Connoisseur*, in which the magazine invited the booksellers to invest £5,000 on behalf of an imaginary reader. Although concerned by the more philistine aspects of the programme, e.g. investors were not even obliged to take their books home (the bookshop would charge a 2% annual management fee for keeping them in store), we took an impartial stand, merely interested to learn how the 'invested' funds would fare. Francis Edwards promised to monitor developments, with twice-yearly reports, over a three to five year period, with the magazine intending to publish interim progress reports. The portfolio read as follows:

Early Printed/Technical

Chippendale (T.), 'The Gentleman and Cabinet-Maker's Director', 1762 (3rd and best edition with the rare dedication page to Prince Henry – which the King ordered to be torn out – left in.) £1,300

Voyages/Travel/Topography

Casati (Major G.), 'Ten years in Equatoria and the return with Emin Pasha', 2 vols., 1891 £65

Coker (J.), 'A Survey of Dorsetshire, 1732 £225

De Long Expedition, 'Our Lost Explorers', 1882 £35

De Long (G.), 'The Voyage of the Jeannette', 2 vols., 1884 £85

Smith (J. E.), 'A Sketch of a Tour on the Continent', 1807 (While old travel books are always in demand, this is also known as an Association Copy because it comes from the library of William Beckford, and contains five pages of his notes.) £240

Lawrence (T. E.), 'Secret Despatches from Arabia' (This copy has an added value because it could also be classified as a Private Press book, being published by the Golden Cockerell Press, one of the outstanding producers of fine books.) £200

Beaglehole (J.), 'Journals of Captain Cook', 5 vols. + folio of plates, 1968–74 (In contrast to every other book in the portfolio, this set is only recently out-of-print, but still in demand as the definitive work will automatically rise in price.) £100

Natural History/Science & Technology

Thorburn (A.), 'British Birds', 4 vols., 1915–16 (Many colour plates in this definitive work; unusual in that it is nicely bound contemporary copy.) £550

Nasmyth (J.), 'The Moon', 1874 £150

Priestley (J.), 'The History and Present State of Discoveries Relating to Vision, Light and Colours', 1772 £250

Pryce (W.), 'Mineralogia Cornubiensis', 1778 £350

Worlidge (J.), 'Systema Agriculturae', 1675 £280

Literature

De Quincey (T.), 'Klosterheim', 1832 £100

Dickens (C.), 'Martin Chuzzlewit' Bound from parts, 1844 £50

Haggard (H. Rider), 'Cleopatra', 1889 £30

Hardy (T.), 'The Well-Beloved', 1897 £50

Kingsley (C.), 'The Water Babies', 1863 £50

Kipling (R.), 'Kim', 1901 £40

Lawrence (D. H.), 'Lady Chatterley's Lover', Florence, 1928 £250

Literature/Illustrated

Cruikshank (G.), 'The Life of Sir John Falstaff', 1858 (An usually fine copy of Cruikshank's drawings.) £100

Bentley (R.), 'Design by Mr. R. Bentley for 6 Poems by Mr. T. Gray', Quarto, 1776 £225

Naval

Burchett (J.), 'A Complete History of the Most Remarkable Transactions at Sea', 1720 £275

Unfortunately, for various reasons unconnected with this scheme, Francis Edwards ran into financial difficulties and was eventually taken over by another firm who did not pursue the investment portfolio programme. However, since the scheme was never tested, I thought it would be an interesting theoretical exercise to assess how the *Connoisseur* portfolio might have worked out. Leaving aside the ambiguity of Francis Edwards' prices and how they were calculated, I wanted an authoritative independent approach, (which rules out friends in the antiquarian trade who might have an axe to grind) and asked Bloomsbury Book Auctions, the fast growing London auction house – in fact, the only one in the UK devoted solely to books. The following figures are their *estimates* of current values, reached without having seen the books – an almost impossible brief, bearing in mind the critical influence of condition. Their figures are based on likely auction prices plus the bookseller's mark-up:

Book	£/$	Profit £/$ (conv. @ $1.45)
Chippendale	1,800/2,610	500/725
Casati	110/159.5	45/65.25
Coker	250/362.5	25/36.25
De Long Exp.	50/72.5	15/21.75
De Long	140/203	55/79.75
Smith	400/580	160/232
Lawrence	275/398.75	75/108.75
Beaglehole	150/217.5	50/72.5
Thorburn	700/1,015	150/217.5

Nasmyth	180/261	30/43.5
Priestley	420/609	170/246.5
Pryce	750/1,087.5	400/580
Worlidge	400/580	120/174
De Quincey	110/159.5	10/14.5
Dickens	80/116	30/43.5
Haggard	30/43.5	same
Hardy	65/94.25	15/21.75
Kingsley	90/130.5	40/58
Kipling	90/130.5	50/72.5
Lawrence	350/507.5	100/145
Cruikshank	350/507.5	250/362.5
Bentley	275/398.75	50/72.5
Burchett	400/580	125/181.25
	7,465/10,824.25	2,465/3,574.25

The appreciation is quite reasonable, even allowing for the fact that the list was made up of 'safe' titles (note the absence of books apt to fluctuate in price, such as modern first editions which might have risen dramatically, but equally may not!) The novelists included have always been collected, and while they cannot compare with the vast prices paid today for their modern counterpart (when there are dust jackets involved), the rise is invariably steady. Similarly the demand for plate books is constant; even when falling to pieces they have their value as 'breakers', and topography will always find buyers, especially as the older titles become more rare. That is not intended as a criticism, since appreciation was the name of the game; merely that Francis Edwards was showing commendable caution with the imaginary reader's money.

However, as the brief was to promote books *as* an investment, comparisons with the performance of other forms, are inevitable. In the same five-year period, using the most common comparisons (with net income reinvested), a Building Society would have realised £7,190 (a 'profit' of £2,190); National Savings Certificates £7,700 (£2,700), and Unit Trusts £14,810 (figures supplied by the Unit Trust Association covering a middle range spread of UK investments). Whichever way one interprets these performances, it is clear that in investment terms alone, books leave much to be desired. The bibliophile buying the same portfolio of books (!) because he happened to collect that particular mix, is not concerned with 'performance'; he has the satisfaction of possessing books he has no intention of selling.

Even the most astute dealer needs all his or her wits and energy to compete successfully in today's more aggressive markets. I know of one who has probably forgotten more about the book business than many of his colleagues will ever learn, but who has been obliged through ill-health to cut down on the scale of his activities. As part of that process, the sale of some real estate linked to the business resulted in a modest nest-egg for the future. If the investment potential of books was as great as some imagine, there can be no doubt that he would have known what to buy to 'lay down'; but the money went into stocks and shares. If an expert makes that choice, what chance is there for the amateur? I would concede that had this man been fully fit and a little younger, he might have acted differently – but it is one thing to trade actively, using instinctive skill and judgement as well as knowledge; another to 'dabble' from the sidelines.

Of course, one can always point to spectacular profits on certain books, particularly modern first editions; indeed, there would be no book trade if it were not possible to buy and sell at a profit. There are countless trade anecdotes about profit margins of which various dealers will swear they know the origin – until pressed for evidence – so here is another apocryphal story about an American bookseller who put a price tag of $130,000 and 50 cents on a certain book. The customer was perfectly happy to pay the asking price, but queried the extra 50 cents Why couldn't he make it a round figure? The dealer declined, explaining that he wanted to make a straight $100,000 on the transaction!

But even when dealers who live in the market place make mistakes, the collector must be more vulnerable. There has to be an incentive, other than financial. I suggest, for example, that *in general* seventeenth century books are currently undervalued. For obvious reasons, material from the sixteenth century and earlier are in demand for their rarity, apart from their intrinsic individual value, while those of the eighteenth and nineteenth centuries retain their interest for different reasons. This seems to leave the seventeenth century somewhat in limbo, and I am constantly surprised how cheaply many books from this period can be bought. But equally, one of the reasons (if you'll forgive a sweeping generalisation) is that, in the main, general interest seventeenth century books are rather ordinary – and for that reason I cannot see the point in starting a collection. Even if one could spare several thousand pounds, and 'forget' it for twenty or thirty years – in which case you *might* hit the jackpot – we have seen that in pure investment terms there are better gambles to be made. If, on the other hand, we have a particular interest in the period, that is another matter.

Undoubtedly the biggest impact in recent years has been made by modern first editions. Who hasn't heard of the copy of (say) *Casino Royale,* bought for £1.50 one day and eventually fetching £2,000? But people forget that was no ordinary first edition. Admittedly, these things happen, but as rarely as finding any form of treasure in an attic or cellar, as any collector knows. Naturally, as people become more aware of prices that can be attained (when *all* the ingredients are there) they will be that much more careful with their books, and especially dust jackets. But books straight from the publisher can arrive in the shops with dust jackets already marked, scratched or even chipped in transit, immediately detracting from the book's value to the collector.

There is a painfully funny story about an English bookdealer (this one *is* true, but I haven't used his name in case the scars are still fresh), who was so determined to keep his personal collection of George Orwell firsts with jackets in pristine condition, that he refused to stand them on bookshelves; he laid them on their backs in cardboard boxes from the supermarket. To the privileged few he would occasionally open the boxes and allow them to peep, but not touch. But one day a new houseproud girl friend who had not yet been given that opportunity decided that the unsightly boxes were taking up too much room – and gave them to the dustmen. Our unfortunate hero gave chase in his car, but dustcarts these days come equipped with a grinding mechanism . . .

Even more valuable than first editions are proof copies or other pre-published material, such as original manuscripts or handwritten notes – a fashion created in scholastic innocence by the Humanities Research Center of the University of Texas in the early 1960s (see Chapter 5) without realising what they were starting! But the same collecting criteria apply – the main interest being in the early novels and then, obviously, only of the fashionable authors. Proofs are used by sales reps, and as review copies for journals with a long lead time, but most publishers can only justify the bother with potentially major prospects. There was a time when a large number of novels were available in proof form, but 90% of these are worthless to the investor and even to the collector, unless he/she happens to be interested in that author.

As modern firsts continue to come on to the market, it may only be a matter of time before the bubble shrinks and even bursts for all but the 'top end' of the market – where there will always be a demand for perfection, and the rare and unusual. Meanwhile, too many dealers are chasing ordinary titles at inflated prices across a wide spectrum of authors. Many of these writers will go out of fashion in collecting terms (no loss to them since they only get royalties on books in print), and the genre will be like any other area of collecting.

Predicting 'fashion' is a gamble, because the guidelines are so vague. It may be as simple as changing literary tastes at different periods, which is why once-collected authors like John Galsworthy, Hugh Walpole and G. B. Shaw have gone out of fashion (although some of Shaw's earlier works still fetch good prices) but often there is no apparent reason. It has little to do with literary talent: writers of quality such as Evelyn Waugh, George Orwell, Graham Greene and John Fowles remain in demand – but no more than Ian Fleming, Agatha Christie and Dorothy Sayers, authors of more questionable merit. Without doubt, interest in Fleming and early Christie was sparked by film and television adaptations, which have played a significant part in their elevated status – most belated in the case of the ladies, where the interest has also been fuelled by the relatively sudden obsession with dust jackets.

More intriguing is the comparison between authors of similar standing. The works of G. A. Henty, writer of adventure stories for boys, remain in demand after almost a hundred years and will probably remain so for the next hundred especially as the condition of the original editions continues to deteriorate. Interest in Henty is understandable yet similar writers, such as Mayne Reid and

Westerman are practically ignored. It may have something to do with the biographies written on Henty, adding to his popularity – being in a small way the forerunner of today's TV chat programme which can turn an author into a best seller overnight. Illustrations and eye-catching bindings were another factor, but with today's writers comparing literary styles, what makes John Le Carré and Dick Francis more collectable than (say) Frederick Forsyth and John D. MacDonald? All are first class in the genre.

Interestingly enough, an author's popularity is no longer a handicap. At one time the critic's definition of genius was the poet who died after one privately printed edition sold a dozen copies, while professionals like J. B. Priestley were dismissed as hacks merely because they were prolific. For years, collectors seemed to follow the establishment's lead, but recently that has all changed; there is far less snobbishness. Indeed, we are in danger of going to the other extreme with the arrival of a new Sunday Express £20,000 literary prize launched partly because the £15,000 Booker winners do not have sufficient 'popular' appeal. Collectors in the United States (where these fashions usually start) are prepared to give an arm and a leg for proof copies of Stephen King's enormously popular horror stories, at a time when the royalty advances on his later novels were of record-breaking proportions. His early first editions are also in great demand because, obviously, the print runs in those days were much smaller. Now, King and some of his contemporaries have enough clout to insist that new titles have special limited editions (usually in special bindings) as well as the normal massive run, so that they too can also benefit rightly from the collectors' interest.

King's proximity to the occult and science fiction genre reminds me that this may well be one area in which collecting 'norms' do not apply. The surprise to me in prices achieved by the 1986 sale in California of what was probably the largest auction of SF and Fantasy rare and first editions ever held (4,000 items in 1,400 lots) – a 'highlight' collection from specialist Los Angeles dealer, Barry R. Levin – was the relative lack of interest in the very old books of the genre. One would generally expect early books in any sphere to be sought after, yet the opposite was true. As a former collector of SF I was fascinated by three titles in particular. What would *you* think was a fair value for the following, all in very good condition:

(1) Daniel Defoe's *The Consolidator*, a 1705 political satire of a voyage to the moon in a feathered spacecraft?

(2) Paltock (Robert), *The Life and Adventures of Peter Wilkins, A Cornishman*, two volumes with six copper engraved plates after Boitard, London 1751?

(3) Wilkins (John), *The Discovery of a New World, Or, A Discourse Tending to Prove, That 'Tis Probable There May Be Another Habitable World In The Moon, etc*, London 1640 (two parts in one; the first a 3rd edition, the second a 1st edition)?

The answers, in order, are $300 (estimate $300–$500); $450 (estimate $600–$900); and $375 (estimate $400–$500).

Returning to Stephen King, such is his current appeal that he outstripped one of the great names of modern SF, Ray Bradbury, in what were two strangely similar lots. King's signed *Firestarter*, one of twenty-six lettered copies in aluminiumised asbestos coated cloth with leather label on front cover, was knocked down at $2,250 compared with Bradbury's signed *Fahrenheit 451*, one of 200 numbered copies, also in asbestos boards which reached $1,500, his lowest auction price in years. Yet Barry Levin was not surprised. 'It may have something to do with being thought to be only as good as your last book. Bradbury has been going out of fashion for the past five or six years; with the exception of one or two books, his prices have been softening or declining. He has not done any work of importance for more years than some of our younger collectors have been alive – while King comes out with one blockbuster after another.'

On the apparent absence of interest in early SF books, Mr Levin adds: 'Many collectors who have reached an age and economic bracket where collecting first editions is feasible, started out as 'fans' or at least avid readers. As they became aware of first and limited editions they tended to start buying those authors they knew and loved in their youth, more than books of broader appeal. They also tend to pick up on what is trendy, such as King.'

The value of acquiring one's own knowledge of the subject cannot be over-emphasised, and this is part of the fun of collecting. The person more interested in 'Investment' is more inclined to rely on the advice of his bookdealer, which is usually valid – but not necessarily so if that person is relatively new to the trade, or if he/she is a general bookseller who cannot possibly keep abreast of developments in specialist areas. Indeed, many specialist collectors are more knowledgeable in their fields than the dealers from whom they buy.

But there is more to acquiring knowledge than in reading reference books because although the information contained can be useful 90% of the time, there are inevitable errors in print which are repeated by writers unable (or too lazy) to check, and which eventually become accepted as fact. In my days as a journalist I interviewed a man who won consistently on the football pools by concentrating on the lower odds of forecasts, in which skill and judgement have a greater role. He did not just read form in the sports pages; he went to the trouble of telephoning the soccer clubs to ask the progress of injured players because of the big difference their availability made to the team.

Newspapers and gossip columnists can be a useful source of information, such as when Richard Adams (*Watership Down*), published *The Girl in a Swing* in 1980 and used the name of a real person as one of his characters. Adams was threatened with a lawsuit which resulted in copies being withdrawn after review copies had already gone out. The furore made the papers, and a number of shrewd people held on to their copies – to their profit, because one of the few original versions (with dust jacket) still around is worth in the region of £120, while the authorised first edition in similar condition fetches less than £10. Adams is yet another example of an author who, in collecting terms, promised much but whose books (apart from *Watership Down*) attract little interest.

Any unforeseen restriction on the number of copies available is the name of the game. In Andrew Block's excellent *Book Collector's Vade Mecum* his chapter on modern first editions takes in a number of nineteenth century authors, drawing attention in the case of Matthew Arnold, to the rarity of his *Empedocles on Etna*, published in 1852, and withdrawn from circulation before fifty copies were sold. On reading that passage some years ago I made a point of searching for a copy – and many years later it still eludes me, yet its value is anyone's guess since Arnold is no longer a 'fashionable' author.

Andrew Block was no writer, but the attraction of his style was that he wrote from personal experience. This is what he said about George Moore: '. . . His first work is so rare that even Mr Moore himself did not remember what it was like. It is called *Worldliness: A Comedy in Three Acts*, and was published in pink wrappers in 1874. His first *known* work is *Flowers of Passion* issued by Provost in 1878 . . . *Pagan Poems* was published by Newman in 1881. The author tore the title page out of every copy he could lay his hands on, so that any copy with the printed title page is extremely rare. Yet I have actually had a copy of this work with the author's initials, G.M., in his handwriting at the bottom right hand corner of the title page . . .'

Those authors are, of course, typical of the way fashions change but the collector who backs his judgement by concentrating on writers he/she admires has nothing to lose. In an age of 'hype' it is possible to promote a fashion. It only needs a handful of collectors to start a trend for interest to snowball. The patterns are clear if one observes trade journals where the rise in prices for modern first editions can be clearly plotted over a given period. It is usually the American collector who starts the ball rolling (Stephen King being a typical example), being prepared to pay higher prices for better copies and since in the case of British writers a book is assumed to have been published first in the UK, they approach British booksellers in their quest. As most dealers tend to follow fashion, rather than try to anticipate it, an interest is developed as they buy from and sell to each other. By the time the average collector wakes up, prices have soared. Even if interest is not maintained, it may take a year or so for the momentum to die down.

Incidentally, the assumption that an author is published first in his own country can be misleading and it may occasionally be worth checking. In the case of collected authors, automatically published on both sides of the Atlantic (e.g. John Fowles), a bibliography is often available, but in most cases the collector cannot be sure. Because of an interest in biblio-mysteries, I discovered that my own crime novels featuring a bookseller-detective, Matthew Coll, were collected in the United States, so that there was an interest in the first editions (the American editions usually being reprinted from the original plates). However, in 1984, when sterling was very weak against the dollar, my American publishers decided it made sense to have their copies produced in the UK – the copies being identical apart from the publisher's imprint on spine and title page. On this occasion, because of the way publisher's programmes are planned, the American edition was issued first, and as such was the true first edition – the English version followed a month later. However, an excellent preview in *Publishers Weekly* meant that a second impression was ordered, and this was done by sending for the plates and reprinting and binding in the States to the slightly larger American format. The problem from the collector's point of view is that, to save money, the publishers did not bother to alter the plate and add 'second impression', so that anyone not knowing the background could be misled into believing there were three different first editions.

There are guidelines based on precedent, but no such thing as a 'right' or 'wrong' price for any out-of-print book; a collector is usually prepared to pay what it is worth to him/her. If that book is well written, illustrated, printed and bound, the chances are that it has an intrinsic value in its own right, irrespective of market values; and that applies across a broad range of subjects and categories. It is an appreciation that comes naturally to the book lover, helping develop what might be called 'collecting judgement'. Knowledge is important, not only in identifying different editions, but in guiding that more-or-less instinctive judgement in the right direction.

There are parallels with life where important decisions are made on the basis of knowledge acquired in one way or another. In deciding on a career, for example, we might think that people have a vested interest in three main areas: birth, survival and death – and that these will always provide a living for people selling into those markets. Much the same applies to books, for there are collectors interested in books on babies and children; in food, fitness and fashion, and if not burial itself, then certainly spiritualism, the occult and the unknown. But not everything is as logical. In view of the enormous interest in sex, many of us would be surprised to learn that collectors of erotica are relatively few.

One of the reasons is that, overall, much of the early material is 'tame' by comparison with recently published more lurid pornography, and jaded palates find little of interest in such older publications, if they can be found – unless those books have some special merit, such as illustrations by exceptional artists, such as Beardsley, Rowlandson, von Bayros, Avril, or Sartori, or attractively produced limited editions. The quality of the illustrations of Francois Boucher (1703–70), for example, a friend and protegé of Mme de Pompadour, is demonstrated by the record price of $1.2M at auction in New York early in 1987 for his mildly erotic painting 'A Boy and Girl Blowing Bubbles', which had been estimated to fetch £250,000–£300,000. A second, 'An Allegory of Painting', featuring a girl déshabillé sketching a classical bust reached a mere £582,781! The other reason, of course, is that much of the early material is housed in libraries and museums, and there are only a handful of collections in this category remaining in private hands. The shortage of 'desirable' material is demonstrated by the relative absence of specialist dealers.

In other words, erotica is little different to many other categories, and collected – if the subject appeals – for the rarity of its antiquarian editions, or for the aesthetic qualities of certain other material more easily obtainable – which brings us back to what collecting is all about. Illustrated books have always been sought after, and if those illustrated by fashionable artists like Rackham and Dulac have peaked, then it surely heralds the opportunity to back one's judgement with a lesser known artist whose work is especially appealing to us. Childrens' classics are a rich source, and prices for out-of-print titles illustrated e.g. by Errol le Cain, have already risen sharply.

Prices are usually dictated by demand and although, as I have said, these can be artificially stimulated, many bibliophiles collect books in areas so specialist there can be no demand, because few people are even aware of their existence. At the premises of a New York dealer I once saw a collection of books bound in animal skins (one in human skin); when the owner died, obviously it was not easy to find a kindred spirit with the same collecting interests. How many people do you know who might be interested in buying a collection on fleas, or on the sex-life of dinosaurs? Now he's being ridiculous, I can imagine some of you thinking; at least, those who haven't come across *Bizarre Books*, by Russell Ash and Brian Lake (Macmillan 1985), which brought to our attention hundreds of crazy or dud but genuine titles, such as *Teach Yourself Alcoholism*; *Animals as Criminals*; *The psychic power of Ants*; *Boldness with Bananas*; *The injurious effects of Bicycles*; *Electrically induced Cholera*; *Sex after Death*; *Hairy Ear Rims*; *The History and Romance of Elastic Webbing*; *The Benefits of Farting Explained*; *Intimacy with a Fly*; *Groping*; *Eat Your House*; and *How to Avoid Intercourse With Your Unfriendly Car Mechanic*.

As the authors acknowledge, there are a number of people interested in books in this fascinating category, but what such collections would fetch on the open market is anyone's guess; indeed, this more than anything else separates the genuine collector from the person motivated by investment considerations who, in all probability, would fail to understand the appeal!

Four

'IF I WERE A RICH MAN' – COLLECTORS

In collecting terms, the reputations of 'giants' like Sir Thomas Phillipps and J. Pierpoint Morgan soar like the Statue of Liberty over the life-size deposits of marble and bronze that commemorate the passing of lesser mortals. Books have been written about their achievements, and it must be admitted that society owes a debt of gratitude for the wealth of rare manuscripts and printed books to which we now have access.

But, when one analyses those magnificent private libraries, what did their founders accomplish that some of us might not have matched – given the same almost unlimited funds? If you'll pardon a sweeping over-simplification, 'all' they had to do was to declare an interest – and merely sign the cheques! I am not complaining. It is, after all, a fact that throughout history major collectors in all the arts have been the richest men and women; in Europe frequently emperors and kings.

Today there are thousands of book collectors, most of us with serious intentions, but because of our financial limitations – which make us unpretentious, occasionally diffident, at times even passive – we don't *go* for something because we don't think much of our chances. But sprinkled among us are the exceptions – men and women of quite modest means who refuse to accept the narrower parameters of their 'status', and who compensate in hard work and ingenuity what they lack in finances. It is easy to conjure up glib phrases like 'detective work', but what is that but – as any police officer will tell you – a formula comprising two parts knowledge, two parts instinct or inspiration and three parts patient research and legwork. The other essential ingredient is luck, although often by adopting the right positive approach, we make our own luck.

This chapter is devoted to such people. My two most spectacular examples are men who do not actually collect for themselves – indeed, Hugh Macmillan works for the Archives Office of the Province of Ontario – but the qualities displayed are an inspiration to those of us who do. In fact, although Macmillan gets paid to do what other collectors do for love, the same might be said of all librarians or archivists – but no other Government official in the world can have recovered such a vast treasure trove of historical artefacts as Hugh. He has been doing the job for twenty-three years, and in 1984 was awarded a Doctor in Letters degree by the Laurentian University of Sudbury, Ontario 'in recognition of the contribution made to the cultural, historical and recreational life of Canada.' To maintain this incredible track record he travels about 48,000 kilometres every year (mainly in Canada, but also the United States and Europe) in search of manuscripts and books (among other artefacts) which might be deteriorating in some damp cellar or attic, or even through mischance housed in the wrong library. His methods of transport vary from helicopter to snowshoes, snowmobile to canoe. Not for nothing is he known as the Sherlock Holmes of North America.

It all began in 1964 when he was given a roving commission – the job was new so it was on a year's trial basis – since when he had built up such a momentum of activity that things just 'happen' around him. Hugh's restless energy puts me in mind of a human dynamo who generates so much electricity that he seems to attract what he wants – and anything else – like a magnet. When we first met a few years ago, I was living in North London. Invited to my home Hugh telephoned to explain he had been delayed – at a police station. The reason, it transpired, was that he was relaxing for once – doing the rubbernecking tourist bit at the Tower of London – when another overseas visitor screamed that someone had snatched her handbag. Hugh looked up and saw the thief racing in his direction. Imagine one's own instincts in such a situation? If we are truly honest most would admit to being paralysed by indecision – until the thief had disappeared. Macmillan stuck out a foot, and as the man went sprawling, sat on him until a police officer arrived. To complete the picture I should point out that Hugh was not far off sixty at the time, had a grizzly white beard, and he stands no more than 5ft 7inches tall, but – as the thief discovered to his loss, our hero is built like a barrel and is as strong as a buffalo.

Not, you will agree, the image of a scholarly civil servant whose main interests in life are history and genealogy, but typical of a larger-than-life 'loner' whose successful track record has been coloured on more than one occasion by some form of controversy. In the best fictional detective tradition he has had to find his own way out of trouble – such as the time he was on the trail of a long run of pre-World War I file copies of a weekly newspaper which had gone into liquidation years before following a disastrous fire. The owner of the now defunct newspaper refused to give or sell the old file copies. (I should explain here that material is acquired in two ways – whenever possible, relying on Macmillan's charm and powers of persuasion, as a gift, which may be tax deductible*, or by conventional purchase on a limited budget.)

For once Macmillan's charm let him down, but eventually he tracked down the newspaper's printer who had since moved to Syracuse, in New York State. This time he was in luck because the printer turned out to be a collector who had acquired a ten-year run of the newspapers when the owner had ordered him to take the fire damaged files to the local refuse dump for destruction. At the dump he examined the files more carefully and found that although the outsides were charred most of the newspapers were undamaged.

In due course, the acquisition was announced, but the newspaper owner claimed that the files had been stolen. When receipts were produced, he claimed that the Archives and the printer were in collusion – that he had never given orders for the files to be taken off the premises. Macmillan trusted the printer but had no proof so he had to find some. Revisiting the scene of the fire, he decided to consult contemporary reports of the blaze, if they still existed. He found what he wanted in the back files of the town's

---

*A system long overdue in Europe in which someone donating something of artistic value to the State, can have the value of the gift offset against tax. The scheme was introduced by the Federal Government of Canada in 1976 and means in effect that a Class A institution, such as the Provinces Archives, can on its own authority issue such a donor with a certificate offsetting up to $1,000 against the person's tax. Amounts higher than $1,000 need the authorisation of an independent board of experts.

other, surviving newspaper. Meriting a prominent coverage was an eye-witness account by a person of the utmost authority – the owner of the unfortunate rival newspaper – in which he reported giving instructions for the files to be dumped.

On another occasion a newspaper headlined the story of a truck load of old Quarter Session court records 'stolen' from Fort Malden in Essex County, just across the river from Detroit (an old British fort now owned by the Federal Government) causing questions to be raised in Parliament. The paper published a retraction when Macmillan produced documents proving his authorisation to remove the documents.

In addition to 'legwork' and his instinctive 'noseyness', part of Macmillan's secret is in cultivating people all over the world who have a particular interest in history, on the reasonable assumption that if he passes on something of interest to them, they will try to reciprocate when the opportunity arises. This is how he gets many of his leads. Although he has obtained many rare books in his travels, the most exciting 'finds' have been letters and manuscript material, such as the correspondence between Rev. Egerton Ryerson Young, a dogsled missionary, and Jack London in which the novelist was accused of plagiarising material from the missionary's memoirs, *My Dogs In The Northland*, for the best seller, *The Call of the Wild*. Another aggressive letter was from Thomas Connon, the Canadian who in 1890 invented the world's first panoramic camera, threatening to sue George Eastman, founder of Kodak for stealing his invention.

Persistence is another invaluable Macmillan quality. Having evidence that somewhere in the courthouse in Brockville, were old district Quarter Session records, he refused to be put off when the clerk told him he was wasting his time, and ridiculed a suggestion that the attic might be worth investigating. In fact, when Macmillan borrowed a ladder, all he found initially was a thick layer of pigeon droppings, but undeterred he returned with a shovel and started to dig – to uncover twenty-seven cases containing the records.

Another time, he persuaded the Canadian prospector and explorer, Murray Watts to hand over papers relating to the mines he had discovered, developed and co-owned from the northern tip of Alaska in the west to Baffin Island in the east. When first approached, Watts declared that he had no time for civil servants. But Macmillan not only does not look like a civil servant, his early days make him sound like a character from a Jack London novel, and he was able to talk about his experiences as a cowboy, 'bronco-busting' in Alberta, and as a deckhand aboard an old sealing schooner off the coast of British Columbia. Having gained the old man's grudging approval he was able to start negotiations, pointing out that as Canada's foremost living Arctic explorer Watts had a duty to posterity. Despite his guile and quick wits, Hugh might have conceded defeat until one day he mentioned the fact that his great-uncle was the legendary Matthew McConkey who had won a hotel in a poker game. It was the clincher. 'Well, anybody related to Mat (sic) Conkey can't be all bad!', the mining magnate announced. The result was 400 large cardboard boxes of diaries and correspondence. In return, Watts received a tax-deduction certificate to the value of $24,000.

In contrast, Hugh has stumbled on many of his acquisitions by accident, if that is what might be called being in the right place at the right time. In 1986 he just 'popped in the car' to visit a friend a mere 400 miles away, to collect some military books he had lent the man. On arrival he was shown a bulky tome brought to Canada by the friend's grandfather in 1870 – *The Statutes of Scotland* of 1604. On another occasion, visiting Andrew MacLean, owner of the weekly *Seaforth Expositor,* to accept the gift of an ancestor's survey records, his natural inquisitiveness led him to a large volume of old newspapers, which turned out to be very rare copies of the *Edinburgh Whig* between 1804 and 1820.

Such discoveries outside the immediate interest of the Ontario Archives have benefitted other libraries and institutions particularly in Scotland, in the course of which he has also recovered books and documents which had gone 'missing' from their original homes. The most spectacular treasure trove was when he heard of a collection of Canadiana, gathered by the Rev. John MacKechnie, minister and scholar – but which turned out to be predominantly Scottish material. In addition to many scholarly books were vellum and parchment material dating back to the fourteenth century which he obtained for the University of Guelph, which has the largest collection of books on Scotland anywhere outside that country.

However, on closer examination it was suspected that the Rev. MacKechnie had no right to most of his collection. It seems that MacKechnie, author of a definitive bibliography on Gaelic manuscripts, had during his researches been given access to the private archives on various large estates. Many of the manuscripts of particular interest to him had been taken home for further study – and forgotten – and since in most cases the archives had not been properly catalogued they were not missed. In the early 1960s the Rev. MacKechnie left his job at a Scottish university to join his daughter in Canada, becoming minister at a small Presbyterian church at Dunvegan, in Glengarry County but he missed his academic work and left the church to start writing again. To support himself, he was obliged to start selling his collection, and many documents found their way into the libraries of American universities. It was what remained that Macmillan was given to dispose of by MacKechnie's daughter.

On one of his trips to Scotland Macmillan continued his detective work, calling on likely owners of the missing material such as the Duke of Argyll, although tracing their origins was a lengthy business and eventually he handed the problem over to the experts best equipped for the task – James Galbraith, Deputy Keeper at the Scottish Records Office, a medieval historian, assisted by Patrick Cadell, Keeper of the manuscript department at the National Library of Scotland.

Not every lead has a happy ending. There is the nightmare memory of the woman in Montreal who greeted him at her front door with the words: 'I've saved you a lot of trouble – I went through all those papers you were asking about, and burned the ones that were hard to read . . .'

Macmillan is like no one else I have ever met, but his *style*, and his philosophy, remind me of an American bookseller, Ken Leach who I've written about elsewhere in the book and who, obviously, is not a collector although in his own words an 'accumulator' of material, sometimes for years, before selling. For the past twenty-five years he has been digging in attics, barns and libraries of New England estates, and coming up with more interesting and unrecorded material (eighteenth- and early nineteenth-century ephemera, pamphlets and broadsides) than any of his rivals – often even older items, such as the Massachusetts Sessions Laws of 1670

Advertisements from old newspapers found
by Hugh Macmillan

– **Wanted a wife – genteel english, scotch, or french girl with
money, used to confinement and the keeping of her tongue
(Quebec Gazette 1764)**

Canadians were just as chauvinistic over a century later:

– **Wanted a wife – a girl under 27 from a farm with a little money
as I have none, no redheads and not too thundering big (Emo
River 1887)**

which no one had even heard of, let alone seen! Unfortunately he is
not a collector in the true sense.

As I was saying, Hugh Macmillan is a man out of his time. One
can visualise him as an eighteenth century frontiersman trading
with hostile Indians – offering furs in exchange for the artefacts of
their history. Canon John Fitch, an English country cleric, could
not present a greater contrast. What they have in common is a love
of history and of books. Although the minister's life has been
devoted to the Church, much of his spare time has been committed
to solving the mystery of how the book collections of three parish
libraries simply 'disappeared' – and, more important, trying to
track them down. From the timeless backwaters of Suffolk, he has
traced and sometimes actually recovered missing books in places as
far apart as Australia and the United States. A quarter of a century
later books are still being returned.

Both investigative and recovery operations are fascinating,
although it is the latter which has proved the more successful to
date. However, how the books disappeared, or were stolen, may
never be satisfactorily resolved because country people are
traditionally inhibited about what they regard as their 'personal'
affairs – although Canon Fitch has his theories, particularly in
respect of two clergymen, one of whom might have stepped out of
the pages of a Sherlock Holmes story.

John Fitch has worked in Suffolk as a parson for approaching
forty years since taking a degree in history at Cambridge and,
although always a bibliophile, was barely aware of the existence of
parochial libraries until he helped to organise an exhibition of
church treasures in 1961. The exhibition coincided with a growing

public concern at the increasing number of sales of old church libraries, which led to the formation of a committee to report on the situation in England and Wales. Their work inspired Fitch, then vicar of Reydon (1951–70), to begin cataloguing the Beccles Parish Library, and shortly thereafter the then Bishop of St. Edmundsbury and Ipswich set up the Diocesan Parochial Libraries Committee, of which John Fitch was an original member, becoming chairman. In 1966, he discovered that until c.1890 there had been in the various churches and parsonages in Suffolk, eleven parochial libraries founded between 1590 and 1790. The three which had 'disappeared' were:

Sudbury All Saints, the smallest, with only sixty-two volumes at the outset, was notable only as an example of the libraries set up and sent out by Dr Thomas Bray, the divine and philanthropist who did so much to help the public-library movement in England and America in the late seventeenth and early eighteenth centuries. Dating from 1712, the library comprised only standard works of divinity.

The *Milden* library of over two thousand volumes was left by William Burkitt, Rector of Milden (d.1703) – and Vicar of Dedham, Essex – whose *Expository Notes on the New Testament* were reprinted many times in the eighteenth century. In accordance with the terms of his will, the library remained at Milden Rectory until 1904 when the rector of that time, the Rev. A. F. Rivers, gave it to the Sudbury Archdeaconry Bray Library at Bury St. Edmunds, with a recommendation that the old books be sold and replaced with modern theology more 'useful' to the twentieth century parson! The efforts of Rivers' successor to obtain the books' return were blocked, and the Burkitt books disappeared *en masse*. Only one volume has been traced – to the Houghton Library of Harvard University.

The most intriguing was that of *Brent Eleigh*, a beautiful village of under two hundred people, two miles from Lavenham. The library was founded by the will of Henry Colman, DD, Fellow of Trinity College, Cambridge, Rector of Harpley, Norfolk, and Squire (but not Rector) of Brent Eleigh, who died in 1715. The £1,000 bond of 1720 signed by the then rector, Thurloe, and binding him and his successors to maintain the library according to the terms of Colman's will, survives in the Norfolk and Norwich

Records Office, and attached to it is a complete catalogue closely written on two large parchments, of the 1,700 or so volumes. In 1887 and 1891 the then rector sold the manuscripts – which included Martial's *Epigrams* (fifteenth century) – and all survive. But the printed books, which were not on offer, disappeared without trace some time after 1891.

John Fitch began his search, with the help of friends such as Michael Tupling, librarian at the County Library at Bury St. Edmunds, by directing his attention at libraries and booksellers on both sides of the Atlantic. It has been the tracking down and recovery of items from the Brent Eleigh library that has given Canon Fitch most satisfaction, and by a strange coincidence, he was to leave Brandon in 1980 to become Rector of Brent Eleigh and its three sister parishes (Milden, Monks Eleigh, and Chelsworth) which gave him more direct access to records and to its older parishioners whose memories might reveal a clue or two.

One of the first books to be found, Samuel Newman's *A Concordance of the Holy Scriptures* (Cambridge, 1698) turned up at the Folger Shakespeare Library in Washington, which sent John Fitch a photocopy of Henry Colman's autograph and the manuscript press marks from the inner front cover. This folio volume was bought by Folger from Bernard Quaritch in 1921, and although the lead was followed up it came to nothing.

In 1968 *Oratores veteres* (Paris, 1575) was found in Urbana University Library, Illinois, by which it had been purchased in 1949. Inside was handwritten 'Brent Ely (sic) Library' inscription with class marks. In 1976, the same bookplate was found in a second edition of Samuel Woodford's *Paraphrase of the Psalms of David* (London, 1678) at the University of Glasgow to which it had been donated in 1919 by the Very Rev. James Cooper, then Professor of Ecclesiastical History, and sometimes Moderator of the Church of Scotland. How it came into his possession is not known.

Two other items from the library turned up in the collection of an antiquarian bookseller, G. V. M. Heap. Some years later Mr Heap moved from Somerset to Bury St. Edmunds and became a member of Canon Fitch's committee, and when he died two years ago the two Brent Eleigh books – one a Greek anthology published in 1711 for the use of boys of Westminster School, and the other a

1742 edition of the works of the Greek philosopher, Hierocles – returned to their rightful place (one was purchased; the other donated by Mr Heap's executor).

In 1977 another story emerged in an unexpected place: it was found among the Brent Eleigh manuscripts at the University Library, Cambridge. A librarian had been working on a catalogue of medieval manuscripts and had traced some of them back to Lord William Howard of Carlisle, an enthusiastic collector at the time of Elizabeth I and James I. With the manuscripts acquired at the auction of 1891, was just one book from Brent Eleigh: William Restell's *A Table Collected of the Yeres* (sic) of *Our Lord God and the Years of the Kings of England* (London, 1571). Inside was the 1727 signature of a clergyman, Fane Edge, a descendant of the Fane family, Earls of Westmorland, indicating a connection with the Howards.

Other books traced have a degree of special interest, e.g. *Exercitations anatomicae* (Rotterdam, 1671), by William Harvey, discoverer of blood circulation, which appeared in the University Library, Newcastle-upon-Tyne, and the works of Horace, published by the Cambridge University Press in 1699 in the collection of Mr Peter Scupham, scholar and publisher, of Hitchin, Herts. The value of this item purchased in 1980 for a nominal sum by Canon Fitch's committee is that it was the first major work published by C.U.P. after it had been re-established in 1698 under the auspices and control of the University.

When I wrote *Antiquarian Books: An Insider's Account* (David & Charles, 1978), I referred to Canon Fitch's search suggesting that readers might participate. A year later Dr J. M. Emmerson, of Melbourne, wrote announcing that he had in his possession Sir Robert Filmer's *The Free-holders Inquest* (4th imp 1684) bound with his famous *Patriarche* (1680), complete with Brent Eleigh marks, which had been purchased in London in 1969.

In July 1983 John Fitch received a letter from Ian Jackson of Berkeley, California saying that he had recently bought at auction Joseph Beaumont's *Psyche, or Love's Mystery in XXIV Cantos – the Intercourse betwixt Christ and the Soul* (C.U.P., 2nd edn 1702). It bears the autograph of Susanna Colman, widow and executor of Dr Henry Colman, as well as the usual Brent Ely (sic) inscriptions and shelf mark.

Canon Fitch and his committee realise that most books have 'vanished' for ever; others will be traced but never obtained because they had been purchased in good faith, yet gradually the books are finding their way home. Recently, six more Brent Eleigh books have emerged – in the collection of Mr Don Cumming, of Coulsdon, Surrey, who started book collecting on leaving the navy after World War II and was able to buy some fascinating material at a time when they were incredibly cheap, although the parochial library volumes had been left to him by a collector friend and he does not know how they were originally acquired. In 1984, having got round to cataloguing his early books, paying special attention to provenance, he decided to pay a visit to Brent Eleigh. After meeting John Fitch one thing led to another, and eventually a codicil was added to his will, bequeathing five of the six to the Suffolk Records Office, where the three Brent Eleigh books recovered earlier are kept.

The five are:

Gulielmus Durandus, *Rationale Divinorum Officiorum* (The Rational of Divine Offices), Lugdunum (Lyons) 1516, published by Jacob Hugueton, printed by L. Hyllaire, quarto (very scarce, not even in the British Library catalogue)

Claudius Aelianus (Aelian), *De Historia Animalium* (History of Animals), Lugduni 1562, published Guliel Rouillium octavo

Publius Afer Terentius, *Comoedia Sex* (Six Comedies), Lugduni 1581, 16 mo. (also not identified in British Library catalogue)

Severinus Boethius, *Of the Consolation of Philosophy*, published London 1712 by J. Tonson and J. Round (English translation by Richard, Viscount Preston), octavo

Willam Howell, *Medulla Historiae Anglicanae*, (A Summary of English History), London 1712, octavo

The sixth title: Quintus Horatius Flaccus (Horace), *Opera* (Works of), Lugduni 1561, is left to 'whomsoever of my children may choose to have it, but should neither of them wish to keep it, then it also be bequeathed to the Suffolk Records Office. Interest in this copy is heightened considerably by its provenance. Unlike the others it actually had four owners before going to the Brent Ely (sic) Library, and there is a mystery note on the back flyleaf – a dinner menu, fascinating not only for the food consumed but for the important guests at the dinner, and the identity of the person who copied it down.

The writing refers to the menu on 20 September 1564 when 'Lord Robert, Lord of Warwick and Lord of Huntingdon dined with me'. Mr Cumming, having made a considerable effort to identify the writer is convinced that the three guests of honour were Robert Dudley (Lord Robert), Earl of Essex and favourite of Elizabeth I; his brother Ambrose Dudley (Lord of Warwick); and Henry Hastings (Lord of Huntingdon) married to Catherine, Robert's sister. The evidence from his research – circumstantial, he admits – points to Roger Ascham, tutor and secretary to Queen Elizabeth. Incidentally, there is no indication of the numbers of people at the dinner, but since the menu included quantities of turkey, chicken, capon, venison, veal, beef, lamb, mutton, pheasant, partridge, quail and oysters, it must have been a pretty distinguished gathering!

John Fitch's comprehensive investigations have led him to make a study of former rectors such as the man who died in an asylum in 1921, and was reputed to be a secret opium smoker and brandisher of knives in frequent skirmishes with his wife – although this caricature of villainy was soon eliminated from his enquiries.

There is evidence that books from the library were seen in the village as late as the 1930s. Tantalisingly, a former secretary of the Church Council who had come to the village in 1913 told Canon Fitch that some of the books were *still* in the village, repeating this bombshell on his death-bed a few months ago. 'Nothing on earth would make him divulge their whereabouts,' says John Fitch, 'we are utterly baffled.'

As the older residents die, it seems that any remaining secrets will die with them, but the search for the books that did leave Suffolk will continue for many years to come, although with John Fitch's retirement in 1987, the impetus was bound to flag.

Energy and resourcefulness seems to be the common denominator for 'active' collectors who cannot afford to sit back and wait for dealers to come to them with choice titbits. Dan Laurence, American professor and editor of the multi-volume *Collected Letters of Bernard Shaw* (Dodd, Mead & Co, NY/Max Reinhardt, London), combined all of that with the ingenuity of a detective to amass his impressive Shaw collection, now housed at the University of Guelph (see Chapter 5). The leg work – whether it be advertising in specialist newspapers such as *The Stage* for theatre memorabilia, or rummaging through junk stalls and church bazaars – he takes for granted, but if pressed might concede that it is often his imagination that gives him an edge over his competitors.

While most restrict their searches to bookshops and auction catalogues, Professor Laurence's enquiries also took him outside the bookworld, back into history to find associates of Shaw who might have been in a position to help even indirectly. Through a society of shorthand reporters in London he managed to track down C. H. Norman who had been hired by Shaw to take down his impromptu lectures, and from him obtained pamphlets he had never heard of. Similarly, more than a quarter of a century ago the Fabian Society helped him trace F. Lawson Dodd, a retired dentist then living in Sussex, who had been a member of the Society's executive committee in the early years. Dan Laurence recalls: 'He was then ninety but as bright as they come, and he loaded me down with two or three sacks of papers that contained some of the scarcest items in my collection – and wouldn't take a penny for them.'

In the days when publishers had their own warehouses – in other words, when there was someone around who could actually remember old stock – collectors were occasionally able to turn up unexpected prizes. Years ago, in response to a casual enquiry from me an old warehouseman at what was then G. Bell & Sons produced the two volumes of *Occasional Papers Published for Members of the Samuel Pepys Club*, Chiswick Press 1917 and 1925, limited to 250 copies and exceptionally scarce, having been out of print for at least forty years. The copies were in mint condition and still protected by the original transparent paper wrappers, and when I asked the price he consulted the last catalogue containing the title and made out a bill for £1.50, although as most will appreciate it wasn't just the bargain that made the transaction so memorable. But while my experience was a fluke, Dan Laurence's searches were quite systematic. From visiting the printers of Shaw's works he was rewarded with a variety of material from books to pamphlets and stereotyped – message postcards, and in the basement of a music publisher he found, bundled away in a corner and covered by inches of dust, GBS's mother's song sheets, seventy-five years old – buying them for a few shillings.

Like all collectors, the professor had accumulated a wealth of duplicate material, but his use of those duplicates is a lesson to many of us. Rather than trying to make a quick profit, he usually exchanged the rarest 'spare' items with fellow collectors or even libraries. Although in the earlier days when he was very short of money he would buy a small collection for one or two items he particularly wanted and recoup his outlay by selling the rest to a dealer, he discovered that even realising good prices did not help contribute to his never ending quest, whereas a straight 'swop' might bring in something exciting.

Colin Wilson, one of Britain's outstanding writers of the second half of this century, will be remembered long after many of the names currently more 'fashionable' among collectors (although his early titles are still in demand). When *The Outsider* was published in 1956 it was immediately recognised as a work of major importance. Accepted as something of a phenomenon by critics and scholars, as well as the reading public, Wilson's success coincided with what was conjured up by the media as the age of the 'angry' young men; he became a celebrity as well as 'serious' writer.

It was not to last. For a young man in the public eye he had too high a profile, and this made him a sitting target for the media. More important, as a literary figure he was too talented and too versatile. Able to write brilliantly in so many difficult areas, he churned out material with a proficiency that disturbed the literary establishment, always suspicious of a possible genius who persists in using his right hand to pound a typewriter when he should be clutching it to a fevered brow. It may be true that in keeping to such an intensive schedule, he did not always stop to 'polish' a manuscript which might have fallen short of his own standards, but nothing can detract from his remarkable talent. Meanwhile, interspersed with the occasional best seller, sales have consistently been steady. Significantly, he continues to be 're-discovered' by successive generations – noticeably so in the mid 1980s – and I suspect this pattern will be maintained well into the next century.

All this is by way of a lead-in to Colin Wilson the collector, because in some ways the wide ranging interests of his books reflects his diversity as a writer. It doesn't follow that authors need to have an affinity with other people's books but in my experience the majority do. Among them, some collect seriously but Wilson's style is instinctive, clutching at everything he wants to read and not really terribly concerned whether it was a bargain or overpriced. Apart from its size, his home in Cornwall is a ringer for Arnold Bennett's *Riceyman Steps* where books spill from every nook, cranny and even the bath. Wilson is more disciplined – slightly – with approaching 30,000 books occupying eight large rooms in the house, over-flowing into corridors, and five other rooms outside, including a library shed. The irony of this apparent chaos is that his wife, Joy, was trained as a librarian. Her problem is that she is a bibliophile too!

Undoubtedly, one of the reasons the library is so large is that, living off the beaten track, Wilson needs the equivalent of a London Library for immediate access to research material, and his specialist collections are very comprehensive; they include a basement full of occult, 2,000 volumes on real crime, an impressive music section and another more unusual on maths and science (he also has 30,000 records). However, within the subject categories rare first editions rub shoulders with what were once paperbacks, but subsequently rebound by Remploy. Even old and possibly valuable books picked up cheaply at some stage in the past have been re-covered in this way, because Colin is not interested in their monetary value; he wants his books to read, and as such they need to be durable. A collector of the traditional school, he recalls how it began. 'When *The Outsider* first came out and I had a little cash to spare for the first time, I remember the sheer delight of being able to go into secondhand bookshops and buy as many books as I wanted. Again and again I had to park the car somewhere quite close, and stagger out with large cardboard boxes full of books.'

Among all the classics of literature are many ex-library copies, but as I said before, appearance concerns him far less than content. And what is too shabby can always to rebound – even antiquarian material which some believe is sacrosanct and should not be touched – such as his 1684 edition of *An Enquiry Into, And Detection of the Barbarous Murther of the Late Earl of Effex*, in the documentary crime section. However, some of the first editions among 'sets' of many of the great names, T. S. Eliot, H. G. Wells,

W. B. Yeats, D. H. Lawrence and Wyndham Lewis, are quite rare.

Among the more unusual items for which he has a special affection is a small set of six volumes of Charles Dickens' magazine *All The Year Round*, launched in 1858 shortly after *Household Words* came to an end. Colin was particularly anxious to obtain the set because it contained the first printing of *A Day's Ride, A Life's Romance*, by Charles Lever, a novel which had impressed Bernard Shaw so much when he read it in that edition as a boy (Wilson published a study of Shaw in 1969). But the books belonged to Joy's mother who for some unexplained reason disliked them and instructed her daughter to put them in a sale. Joy carried out her instructions, but soon joined in the bidding – and bought them back!

In view of the Wilsons' large circle of writer friends it is hardly surprising that there are a number of signed, dedicated copies; similarly, because of the sheer volume of material in the house there are inevitably many association copies, such as those by the philosopher Samuel Alexander, e.g. *Beauty & Other Forms of Value, Philosophical & Literary Pieces*, and *Art and Instinct* – all of which have the bookplate of Marie Stopes, who was his student and great admirer, and were all inscribed to her from the author. A little volume, *Relics of Shelley* was from the library of Coventry Patmore, distinguished nineteenth-century author and poet, and there are many other examples.

Another writer whose collecting activities are more disciplined, and who epitomises my insistence that the true collector has no thought of selling, is the respected aviation author, Owen Thetford. Owen has an impressive library of over 4,000 novels from the year 1900, but not confined to English and American writers. Like all of us he has memories of great satisfaction – and regret. He would willingly turn back the clock if he could to head off the moment he succumbed to a momentary whim about shelf presentation, which led him to discard all the jackets to his set of first editions of Anthony Powell's *Music of Time* series – at a stroke knocking off hundreds of pounds *at least* off their value (see Chapter 6). Recalling the incident, Thetford concedes, 'Maddening, of course, but as I do not intend to sell them anyway, who cares? I confess though to a feeling of irritation every time I enter a bookshop and see those lovely coloured jackets* winking at me.'

Obviously Owen has kept and treasures his other dust jackets; indeed, as well as the excitement of the chase and discovery, he admits to an aesthetic pleasure from arrangement and the contemplation of book jackets and typographical features. 'Most exciting of all,' he reveals, 'is the consideration that one might well be building a sort of time capsule representing an informed but very personal evaluation of the significant books in a reasonably wide survey in the twentieth century.'

Owen's constructive approach to collecting provides an object lesson, and I am passing on certain tips on *what* to collect, which have some educational value to all but the most knowledgeable first edition buff. For obvious reasons, he began with aviation books – the collection today running to some 2,000 volumes, but it was through reading many of the novels and non-fiction of H. G. Wells in the 1940s, that his interest in general literature was fired, and in particular the modern novel. The pleasures of discovering and enjoying new authors has always been associated for him with the parallel study of relevant criticism and literary history and biography which forms an important section of the collection. To absorb certain key works of criticism or literary history *before* plunging into the original creative work can enhance the pleasure 'a hundred-fold' by intensifying perception and understanding.

The 'groundwork' for the collection on modern writing was laid with a fair cross-section of titles in the Dent Everyman Library (covering the classic English and European novelists and dramatists); these were supplemented by Collins and Oxford Classics. By then he had moved into the modern English novel by way of Wells, Bennett and Galsworthy read purely for pleasure but soon augmented by some critical works which aroused his desire to investigate the entire field of modern fiction across national boundaries. These were Frank Swinnerton's *The Georgian Literary Scene*, and Edwin Muir's *The Present Age from 1920* in the Cresset Press series on English literature. Later invaluable background books proved to be Walter Allen's *Tradition and Dream*, 1964; all of V. S. Pritchett's impressionistic criticism, but especially *The*

*On reprints

Living Novel, The Working Novelist, and *Books in General,* Gindin's *Post War British Fiction,* 1962; and the later criticism of Malcolm Bradbury, Anthony Burgess and David Lodge.

Meanwhile Owen Thetford's collection was growing rapidly, to the extent that almost every writer of quality was represented, in first edition, reprint or even paperback. And to show that he is at least aware of the investment aspect he recommends Joseph Connolly's *Modern First Editions,* revised in 1984. H. E. Bates' *The Modern Short Story,* which he describes as 'wonderful and suggestive', led to him setting up another sub-section of fiction, concentrating on attractive single-volume collected short stories of all the established practitioners from A. E. Coppard to V. S. Pritchett and Angus Wilson; his special favourite being William Trevor.

As he progressed to the American novel, the learning process continued with Tony Tanner's *City of Words,* which provides comprehensive coverage from Saul Bellow to John Updike. It is augmented in Thetford's collection by the critical works of Edmund Wilson and Maxwell Geismar, covering the twenties, thirties and forties. For more recent developments he has Winkowitz's *The New American Novel of Manners,* which examines such contemporary writers as Richard Yates, Dan Wakefield and Thomas McGuane.

The interests of many collectors would end there, but Owen Thetford has a growing number of examples of the works of good writers from France, Germany, Italy and Russia, and a 'fringe' collection covering South America, and Japan, although so far this is limited to a separate paperback collection.

Anyone contemplating developing their interest in European literature would do well to follow Owen's lead:

'Indispensable to the starting of the French collection was Bree and Guiton's *An Age of Fiction – Gide to Camus,* (1957)' he explains, 'Naturally, the basis of this section was the celebrated twelve volume Proust translation from Chatto and Windus, but that was soon joined by works of Jules Romains, Martin du Gard, Georges Duhamel, André Malraux, Francois Mauriac's great Catholic novels, George Bernanos, Henry de Montherlant and Jean-Paul Sartre.

Turning to Germany, I found Waidson's *The Modern German Novel* (1959), very useful when establishing a collection to include names which, from Thomas Mann, include Heinrich Böll, Herman Hesse, Gunther Grass, Robert Musil, E. M. Remarque and Arnold Zweig. A sub-section of Central European novels includes the novels of Milan Kundera, Stefan Zweig and Arthur Koestler.

The basis for the Italian section was the book, *Italian Literature*, by Cairns (1977). It includes works by Pirandello, Svevo, Betti, Elsa Morante and Alberto Moravia; however, one must not forget the wonderful Sicilian novel *The Leopard*, by Guissepe di Lampedusa.

Russian literature is a vast subject, but the nineteenth century novels must be studied before going on to the modern Soviet masters. Janko Lavrin's concise *Introduction to the Russian Novel* (1942), started off my collection and got me into Dostoevsky, Tolstoy and Turgenev before I tackled the twentieth century novelists after acquiring the invaluable concise history of *Russian Literature from 1900 to the present day*, by Lindstrom (New York University, 1978). The essential names to collect include Dudintsev, Zinoviev, Terz, Sholokhov and, of course, Solzhenitsyn.'

I am interrupting at this point for a couple of personal asides; the first to point out that many of the works of the talented but as yet lesser known foreign writers can often be picked up cheaply – titles are frequently remaindered – and something I had not mentioned before, but relevant in this context: while the Owen Thetford type of collector is interested primarily in the literary content of his library, others are motivated by the act of collecting itself, i.e. to have a comprehensive collection, and in that case one needs to acquire foreign language editions of the author in question, even if (almost certainly) one cannot understand them; equally, the same applies in reverse if one was interested in a foreign writer, it is essential to get copies in the original edition.

Back to Owen Thetford for a final word: 'In my submission, the key to an understanding of the modern world's sensibilities lies primarily in the novel, which has dominated my collection, but a full understanding is impossible without a parallel concern for modern poetry. The great poets were splendidly produced in the Oxford Standard Authors series, in the larger format, and with this as a base I have added the sumptuous *Collected Hardy* in the Wessex Edition and Faber's *Kipling*, and all the single-volume collected editions of the important names from Auden to Peter Porter.'

Like most serious bibliophiles, Owen has supplementary collections – one on jazz history, the other on cinema history, but it is the modern fiction library for which he has most reason to be proud. Another writer with very similar tastes in modern fiction on an international scale, is Moris Farhi, whose literary talent has already been recognised by a few discerning critics – which means that he too may join the ranks of the 'fashionable' collected authors over the next few years. His library of some 2,000–3,000 modern literature titles has valuable first editions alongside paperbacks and includes an impressive representative coverage of foreign authors; most are English translations, but because he can speak and read Spanish, the collection is especially strong in South American material.

However, rather than cover familiar ground I will tell you about his main specialist collections – one that is relatively unusual for someone who is not a theologian. Moris Farhi became a novelist after spells as an actor and writing TV soap operas, and it was his second book, *The Last of Days* (1984), which really made people sit up. Much of the authenticity of the spiritual qualities of this book, which has the Arab-Israeli struggle as its setting, stems from a deep-rooted understanding of the Middle Eastern religions, Judaism, Christianity and Islam.

Generally, an author working on a book begins with a vague interest in the subject, an interest that is fuelled by his/her initial research – so that the more the writer learns, the more he/she wants to know. In this instance it was the other way about. Authenticity comes from an instinctive 'feel', not from reproducing facts and figures from reference books – the differences between (say) Dick Francis who, as a former jockey, knows more about racing than could ever be assimilated from research, and (say) Dennis Wheatley who ruined the continuity of the story in his otherwise exciting Roger Brook series, by stopping every so often to insert chunks of history almost straight from a text book.

Moris Farhi's interest began with Jewish history, developed through the Jewish-Roman wars, the birth of Christianity and the story of Jesus. The outcome has been a still growing collection of over a thousand books in a relatively narrow area covering 100BC to AD400; as comprehensive as one might find outside a theological college. The incorporation of Islam was inevitable because of the influence of Jewish/Christian doctrine on that religion. A few initially surprising titles in this section include Geoffrey Ashe's *King Arthur's Avalon*, until one remembers the legend of the Holy Grail, and the theory that Jesus visited Cornwall.

There is a romantic facet to this part of Farhi's collection because it was a shared interest in books, and one in particular, that persuaded him he had discovered the ideal wife in Nina, the woman he was to marry. The book was *The Nazarene Gospel Restored*, by Robert Graves and Joshua Podro, an exceptionally scarce title for which he had been searching for several years. Eventually his persistence was rewarded by the purchase of an American edition from a bookseller in the United States. Suspecting that the young lady was sympathetic to his interest in books, on his next visit he explained the reason for his high spirits, upon which she left the room – to return with the English edition *and* a copy of *Jesus in Rome*, the other equally scarce collaboration between Graves and Podro. He was further impressed by the discovery that Podro, a leading Talmudic scholar and author, was Nina's uncle.

In common with Owen Thetford, Moris also has 'minor' collections, although the one on Psychology, which he shares with his wife, who happens to be a psychiatrist, has over 1,000 volumes – which is hardly 'minor' by specialist standards.

It took writers Peter and Iona Opie forty years to assemble what was to become one of the most comprehensive children's libraries in the world. The collection was, of course, invaluable research material for their own books on the history of children's literature, but it was also a labour of love, and every purchase – from their very first eighteenth century chap-book, *The Cheerful Warbler*, which cost 5s (25 pence) to the most expensive single acquisition (£100) for a first edition of Edward Lear's *Book of Nonsense* – gave not only further insight into changing attitudes in society, but immense aesthetic satisfaction.

By the time Peter Opie died in 1982, in addition to 12,000 bound volumes, well over 1,000 paper chap-books, and 4,000 comics and magazines, there was also a fascinating collection of mechanical toys. Bibliophiles would find their own different favourites, but highlights include first editions of *The Lady's New Year's Gift: or, Advice to a Daughter* (1688); *Wind in the Willows*, with a dedication by Kenneth Grahame, and *A Guide for Child and Youth* (1723), all of 3in by 2in, yet finely bound in red morocco, and containing almost everything a child might wish to know, in philosophical as well as educational terms. Individually, the books were worth an estimated total of £1M, but when Iona decided to sell the library in 1986 as an inheritance for her children, her stipulation was that the unique record of children's literature spanning 200 years should not be broken up. The logical home for it was the Bodleian library, which already had a large children's collection, to whom she was prepared to let it go for half the valued price. The Bodleian – allowed two years to raise the money – immediately launched a public appeal and achieved their target with time to spare, thanks to wide support including donations from individual schools and one substantial gift from Japan. Typical of the Bodleian's new 'commerical' philosophy was the decision in 1987 to open its doors to a fee-paying public.

It could be said that books and, ultimately the collection, changed the lives of Peter and Iona Opie. It began early in their married life when, walking in a country field, they found a ladybird which prompted them instinctively to recite the old rhyme: 'Ladybird, Ladybird, fly away home . . .', and then wonder about its origin. At the library, Iona looked it up in Halliwell's *Nursery Rhymes of England* (1842), and realising that a hundred years had elapsed, reasoned there was scope for a new study; the result was, *The Oxford Dictionary of Nursery Rhymes* (1951), which established their reputation. (Their first jointly written book four years earlier was, *I Saw Esau* (Williams & Norgate).) From then on there was a steady stream of useful titles. To assist their research they started buying early children's books, initially concentrating on the eighteenth century, which was Peter's main interest, but inevitably as the collection grew to more than 800 volumes published before 1800, being obliged to cross into the next century.

The individuals mentioned so far have one thing in common – each straddling a broad spectrum of interest even in what might appear to be a single subject (e.g. juvenilia), but there is also the 'vertical' interest, i.e. collecting the works of a single author or historical figure. One of the most unusual in this category is Ronnie Roter, managing director of a London-based public relations company, who collects anything to do with the book or film of *Gone With The Wind*. The interest which began a dozen or so years ago has enabled him to compile one of the largest collections of books and memorabilia, on this narrow theme, in the world, and the only one outside the United States; collecting from a distance giving him an added incentive.

Despite the incredible success of the epic film and Margaret Mitchell's fascinating book, the reason why any person would want to become involved in an exhaustive study of what made it all happen, is not immediately apparent – until one speaks to Ronnie Roter, when it all becomes so logical. It began when a growing awareness of the film and book began to intrude on his subconscious, and he became increasingly intrigued by the relationship between fact and fantasy. The film was the quintessence of Hollywood in the late 1930s, and the end of an era. It had all the right ingredients – a story that was larger than life, and actors who were *stars* in the true sense – yet timing might well have had something to do with its huge success. One of the most important features that captured the imaginations of audiences everywhere was the background of the American Civil War, yet viewed in the context of a new and terrible world war, brought an added poignancy as well as authenticity. It was the juxtaposition of romance and reality which fired Roter's enthusiasm to learn all he could about the subject, from book to film, the lives of the players – the authors, film makers and actors.

In some ways, gathering the books – he has several hundred early editions in several languages was relatively straightforward, because apart from the challenge of the out-of-print copies, whenever a new title throwing any light on the legend is published, he is able to buy it at source. Like most collectors, Ronnie automatically goes for first editions on both sides of the Atlantic, and whereas in fiction the differences are usually negligible or even non-existent, he has been fortunate in obtaining them with

'Bookseller and Author' A coloured aquatint, published in 1784 by L. R. Smith, depicts the thin miserable author trying to persuade the publisher and bookseller to accept a manuscript. (This theme was used again by Rowlandson in a later aquatint of 1797, 'Poet and Bookseller'.) Although Wigstead's name appears on the print as its artist, this probably means that he collaborated with Rowlandson by supplying the idea. Little is known about Wigstead and no drawing by him has survived. (*By permission of Roger Baynton-Williams*)

(*Above*) A *Biblia Pauperum* (Bible of the poor), a very rare 15th century 'block book', ie each page printed from one large wood-block, which was a mostly pictorial version intended for poor parishes of mainly illiterate folk. Sold in 1986 for £148,500 – which was £110,500 more than the price at which the same copy had remained unsold only seven years before. (*Courtesy Sotheby's*). (*Below*) A typical entry in Sir Walter Scott's *Magnum Opus* (*National Library of Scotland*)

(*Above, left*) Almost certainly the jacket that accompanied the banned first edition of Lawrence's *The Rainbow*, and thus worth a small fortune. (*Above, right*) *Stamboul*, one of the scarcer and more desirable Graham Greene jackets. (*Below*) Typical of the plain Gollancz style featuring the skilled use of typography, this rare Orwell jacket (with the first edition it contains) is worth approximately £2,000 (well over double that of the more spectacular *Homage to Catalonia*). (*Courtesy of Rick Gekoski*)

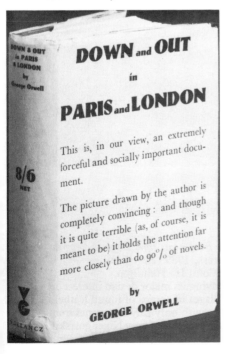

Michael Ayrton's illustration for Jean-Paul Sartre (*Courtesy of David Alexander*)

Edward Bawden's illustration for Traveller's Verse (*Courtesy of David Alexander*)

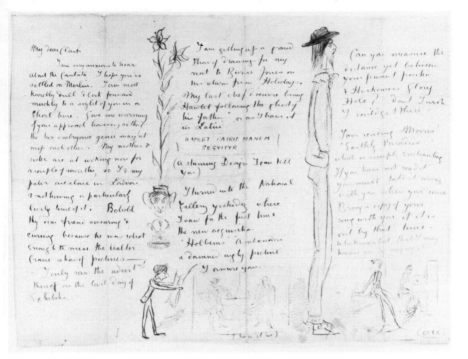

Aubrey Beardsley letter incorporating a poem, a sketch of Whistler's portrait of his mother, plus self caricatures and other drawings. The two page letter offered for sale in December 1986, fetched £9,000 (*Courtesy of Sotheby's*)

The record-breaking 12th century manuscript, *Gospels of Henry the Lion* showing the binding (*Courtesy of Sotheby's*)

significant changes, e.g. the American version of the book about Olivia de Havilland and Joan Fontaine entitled *Sisters,* was published in the United Kingdom as *Olivia and Joan*; while the dust jackets to *A History of the Movies* were different – with the American edition actually featuring *Gone With The Wind.* The books range from umpteen editions of the original, with a variety of dust jackets, and include a copy signed by Margaret Mitchell which gives him special satisfaction because the author had stopped signing copies quite early on – to a large number of biographies of the stars and studies of the film industry. They are supplemented by a large number of magazines, posters, records and other ephemera. In fact the only area in which he has no special interest is the clothes made for the film. 'I like to know the *source* of every item,' he insists, 'the stars had more than one of every item of clothing, so the chance of finding those they actually wore, outside a museum, must be remote.'

Like all collectors, Ronnie regards authenticity as all-important. At an ephemera fair recently he was offered a signed photograph of Clark Gable, complete with its 'original' MGM envelope. But studying the postmark and recognising the still from one of Gable's films, he was able to deduce that there was a time lapse of ten years between envelope and photograph. 'They were offered by the dealer in good faith, and I don't suppose he even looked at the postmark,' he recalls, 'but it's important to me.'

To ensure that there is no possibility of his interests being forgotten, Ronnie keeps in constant touch with all *Gone With The Wind* fan clubs in the United States; indeed, he continues to correspond with people who have been associated in some way with book or film. His most prized possession is a special leather-bound presentation copy of the final shooting script, interleaved with stills from the film, from the producer, David Selznick, to the screenwriter, Sidney Howard.

My spotlight on collectors was not intended to include booksellers who collect, if only for the general assumption that being in the trade it must be so easy. While it cannot be denied that dealers do have certain advantages – such as buying at auction when a mixed lot may include a 'lost' specialist item – the odd title that an ordinary collector would miss – it does not follow that the constant exposure to books day-in-and-out necessarily produces quality as well as quantity. Outside of much embroidered anecdotes, dealers do not constantly stumble on rare books in cellars, attics and under parrot cages; the chances are that anything left to gather dust will not be very exciting. In the main, the most desirable books are bought in the usual way, sometimes even exchanged with colleagues, and, in general it is a case of 'swings and roundabouts'.

However, a couple of booksellers whose personal collections are not for sale are worthy of inclusion as examples of what can be achieved from scratch. George Locke, whose Ferret Fantasy has become Britain's leading specialist in SF and Fantasy – an area which has been only superficially documented. Apart from a hundred or so known writers, and even fewer 'fashionable' ones, there remains a large untapped reservoir of material which currently may be of little value because there is no immediate demand for 'unknown' authors and titles, but which are still useful additions to any collection and may one day themselves be in demand. From his discovery of 'forgotten' books, George Locke has assembled a collection of approaching 4,000 titles, the emphasis on the nineteenth century and books published before 1914, the majority of which are probably unknown to most of us.

Without the benefit of any bibliography or reference book George has simply gone for everything that looked interesting, very often from dusty shelves in neglected corners. Working in such uncharted territory, every title has contributed to the learning process, and over thirty years the knowledge acquired has enabled him to build up a comprehensive picture of the genre. There are still gaps, and he continues to learn from his mistakes – such as the time when, because of his bookselling interests in Victorian fiction, he went to look at a collection of Dickensia at auction. The lot included a desirable Pickwick parody, and glancing through the book he found a passage which roused the collector in his subconscious – a reference to someone looking through a telescope and discovering animals on the moon. Recognising what he hoped was a little known example of Victorian fantasy he bought the collection. Later, having had time to read the passage properly he discovered that the 'animals' were ants in the telescope – intended to be amusing, but certainly not fantasy.

However, by 1980 he was sufficiently an authority on the subject to publish a bibliography of his own collection, in itself an invaluable reference work. Entitled *A Spectrum of Fantasy,* the bibliography demonstrates the way growing collections seem to throw up 'offspring' – smaller specialities within the overall genre, separate categories such as Interplanetary Themes, Lost Races, Future Wars, Utopian Literature, Supernatural and Ghosts, Vampires and Werewolves, Occult Detective (dating from 1828) and Parodies. An updated edition is currently in preparation.

Collecting desirable modern first editions is a simple matter of going to a bookseller and handing over your money. With obscure titles there can be a considerable amount of detective work, and if that book was published in limited edition, it is so much harder. In the 1920s, a SF writer Edward Herron-Allen wrote a collection of short stories called *A Purple Saphire,* which contained a 100-page novella 'The Cheatah Girl'. The story appeared in the list of contents, but at the relevant page instead of the title appeared a brief publisher's apology, regretting its absence. It would seem that the story was considered too 'erotic' to risk publication, which means, amost certainly, acceptable by today's standards.

In the 1930s the author published a paperback limited edition of *The Cheatah Girl,* and in due course this became a challenge for George Locke, who set out to trace a copy. Meeting with no success, he eventually discovered copies at some of the copyright libraries, and finally managed to read the copy at the Bodleian. Thinking it might be worth reprinting he redoubled his efforts to find a copy for himself. In support of his search, George wrote an article for SF enthusiasts and as a result a bookseller who read it, found a copy and put it in his catalogue – which enabled him indirectly, to obtain it. However, in due course, *another* copy emerged – this time with ten illustrations he did not know existed, but which had been commissioned by the author and might have been used in a future edition. Again he managed to buy the copy – although this time for a considerable sum. His current investigation is to trace the artist!

Gerald Coe who died in 1987 was a general antiquarian bookseller whose personal collection of 6,000 titles – Italy, its history and literature – is most unusual for a person whose language is English. Always interested in books, the personal collection was started during World War II, when serving in that country in the Army Medical Corps. 'We landed in Sicily in the dark,' he told me shortly before his death. 'When I woke up, I felt as though I had been there before – it was a very funny feeling.'

His instinctive 'feel' for the Italian way of life was nurtured by opportunities to travel up and down the country with the army, quickly picking up the language. His first 'purchase' was at a bookshop in Bologna when he called the proprietor outside and asked if they could work a 'swap', coming away with *I Promessi Sposi* and *Orlando Furioso* – for forty cigarettes; strictly illegal, of course, but both conspirators were happy.

In 1944, sent to Northern Italy to establish an advance dressing station, at the home of Aurelio Saffi, a powerful statesman at the time of Garibaldi, he was fascinated by the library which consisted entirely of English books; it inspired him to build one on similar lines when he returned to England. Only a small proportion of the collection was actually purchased in Italy during the war or on subsequent visits; indeed, some of the most interesting of this predominantly antiquarian library, came from the homes of the privileged English 'gentlefolk' who had gone on the Grand Tour of Europe and brought back so many literary treasures.

The range of the collection is very wide, from the oldest book *Il Convito* (1544), by Marsilio Ficino, a commentary on the philosopher Plato, to a couple of shelves devoted to books about Mussolini, as a result of which he has corresponded with the dictator's widow, Donna Rachele Mussolini. Literature is, perhaps, most strongly represented, with over a hundred books alone on Dante and his *Divine Comedy*; the most treasured being a five-volume set in vellum printed by Zatta in Venice in 1760. Another very large section is devoted to topography, and one title among the many which hold a special attraction for Gerald Coe is *Historie Dei Veronesi*, by Torelli Saraina, 1586, which he could not find recorded in the Municipal Library of Verona, and which he believed could possibly have been read by Shakespeare who wrote 'Two Gentlemen of Verona' some time after 1589. Some of the volumes have added appeal as association copies, such as a *History of the Revolution of Naples* which once belonged to Florence Nightingale's father, when he was Ambassador in Naples; another is *Estetica*, by Benedetto Croce, which had been bought by Julian Huxley in Verona in 1919.

Five

THE LIBRARY: FROM BOOK REPOSITORY TO CENTRE OF LEARNING

The only part of the bookworld jigsaw we have not yet touched on is the library, yet publishers could not survive without their custom. Complacency being one of the emotional boils on the face of civilised society, it is hardly surprising that the general attitude towards libraries is one of ambivalence. But more puzzling is the positive antagonism felt by some people. Whatever the reason – probably little more than an instinctive kick against what has become another symbol of the Establishment – it continues to manifest itself in the theft or mutilation of books (see Chapter 9). If that sounds paranoic, why is it that the book thief who would not dream of stealing from a somewhat threadbare neighbourhood bookshop, considers the faceless owners of the bigger shops or chains, and libraries, fair game – if they think they can get away with it?

Cynicism towards libraries is not new. Samuel Johnson, admittedly a debunker of virtually everything, maintained: 'No place affords a more striking conviction of the vanity of human hopes than a public library', (*The Rambler*, 1751). I suspect it may have something to do with the way we perceive such outposts of the Establishment, as though a library takes on a human aura, becoming 'someone' we like or dislike. I know a number of people who adopt this totally illogical attitude, quick to find some justification for condemning 'the library'; seldom the real source of the apparent problem, whether it be local authority policy, shortage of funds, or even the short-comings of individual members of staff . . . a carping attitude no more irrational than blaming the British Library for the subversive influence of *Das Kapital*, simply because Karl Marx was allowed to use the Library's Reading Room.

Fortunately, in recent years complaints are usually fairly muted. In the twentieth century, libraries have generally been safe from more violent attacks; even the Nazi book burning parties were held outdoors! In Germany, the burning was mindless vandalism, but there have been occasions when there was at least some practical purpose. In 1814, for example, the British used books from the relatively new Washington Library to set fire to the American capital – another indication that barbarism knows no boundaries. In this instance, it *could* be argued that without the incentive to start over again (because in the following year Congress bought the considerable book collection of Thomas Jefferson as the basis of a new library) the Library of Congress may never have attained its present giant stature.

The Americans got off lightly because in Egypt, the famous ancient Library of Alexandria, suffered a similar fate – twice. The first devastation was caused by Julius Caesar laying siege to the city; in the process, part of a collection of more than a hundred thousand manuscripts assembled over 300 years was destroyed. The second assault was in 642AD when the Arabs conquered the city and their leader, Caliph Omar issued a Catch 22 ultimatum: 'If these writings of the Greeks agree with the book of God, they need not be preserved; if they disagree they are pernicious, and ought to be destroyed.' Again, Omar's action was not completely wanton; the manuscripts were used as fuel for heating the city baths – and there were enough of them to last for six months!

But enough of blood and thunder. In the context of this chapter, we are concerned less with public lending libraries than with the centres of learning. The relationship between collector and library is unusual. Initially in competition over rare items, one may subsequently benefit from the generosity of the other – with bequests from the collector, or – increasingly common with specialist collections – the library playing safe by buying something unique, and even allowing the owner to retain the books during his/her lifetime.

The best reference libraries today provide the most comprehensive source of research material available – housing, in the case of writers, pre-published notes and drafts and ephemera, all of which usually throw fresh light on the subject's craft. Original manuscripts of major literary figures already attract large sums of money, but imagine their worth in the next century when the supply of new material trickles to next-to-nothing as the word processor replaces pen and typewriter. The trend has already begun, although fortunately there will always be authors who are compulsive changers, and continue to amend even printed manuscripts.

The availability of such pre-published material is in itself a controversial issue, unless it is evident that the subject of research would have had no objection to others studying and even reproducing what might be flawed writing, or jotted down random and even personal thoughts. Distinguished writers, such as the English poet Philip Larkin, a very private person, left instructions that his unpublished papers be destroyed – a command with which his executors initially found it impossible to comply. A celebrity in almost any walk of life seems to become public property, forfeiting the right to privacy or even free will. By the nature of his/her work away from the public eye, a writer's privacy seems safe enough, but once dead the 'interests of posterity' may override that person's wishes. In 1981 Gollancz published an 'authorized' biography of Dorothy L. Sayers less than twenty-five years after her death. Forgotten by most was her expressed wish that her papers be destroyed and no biography written for fifty years. It is not for me to criticise the decision to 'jump the gun', especially as the author was given every encouragement by those closest to Ms Sayers. They made their reason known but that does not detract from the fact that she was another very shy (not to say secretive) person, whose wishes were considered – and then overruled.

Such incidents, fortunately infrequent, are not as bad as executors or relatives taking it upon themselves to destroy material which might (in their eyes) reflect unfavourably on the deceased – which is how so much erotica (respectable by today's standards) came to be lost during the Victorian age. Some of that material may have been of questionable quality, but the vandals who destroyed it were seldom the best people to judge. The widow of Sir Richard Burton, translator of the unexpurgated *Arabian Nights*, burned his last great work completed on his death bed – a translation of *The*

Perfumed Garden (and some of the diaries he had kept for twenty-seven years) before he was cold in his coffin. It must be said in her defence that Lady Burton was certainly no hypocrite; a publisher had already offered £6,000 for the new work – a vast amount in 1890.

The more impressive the library, the greater its difficulty in maintaining growth. Bibliographic dinosaurs such as the British Library in London, and Washington's Library of Congress have alarming problems in merely conserving their existing immense holdings, let alone in continuing to buy anything really out of the ordinary. Even in smaller but equally worthy centres, shortage of funds means not only a hold on all but essential buying, but that even gifts of books can be an embarrassment. I know of a couple of older university libraries which were obliged to refuse substantial collections because the only provision was that they should have separate 'accommodation' – something else they do not have; and of several others who have refused the offer of smaller private libraries because the tiny staff does not have the time, on top of routine work, to catalogue them – aware too of the fact that valuable uncatalogued books are the first to be stolen; still others who have accepted such gifts which now lie uncatalogued and virtually forgotten in basements.

The growth pattern of important libraries right down the line has slowed dramatically in recent years – except, it seems, in the United States where some of the 'newer' universities have come from behind to eclipse their more distinguished rivals, to bring new dimensions to the concept of the reference library. Newcomers with ideas above their apparent station will always upset the long established, and in the past quarter of a century there has been consistent criticism of 'irresponsible' buying policies arising from ignorance, supported by too much money. Some of this is prompted by jealousy, although it is true that in certain cases extravagant shopping sprees have been undertaken without thought to a qualified back-up team to 'process' the purchases, which remain uncatalogued for years. However, I can think of a couple of old-established British libraries where important books have been mislaid, sometimes assumed stolen, because there was no proper system for finding them once out of order on the shelves. Similarly, some colleges have overspent in the first flush of enthusiasm when money suddenly becomes available, leaving nothing for other books of greater value to their requirements – let alone funds for essential conservation.

Priorities in Britain's under-financed education system mean that library expenditure on anything outside the immediate requirement for new books – comes at the very end of the begging-bowl queue. Other important libraries, such as that at the Victoria and Albert Museum – once unsurpassed in the arts – are currently being run-down (a trend which may be irreversible). The V & A may deny such allegations, but there is evidence enough in the way enthusiastic key staff have been transferred to other departments. Libraries of most of the older colleges at Oxford and Cambridge, unable to compete in the market place, have narrowed their horizons dramatically and tend to concentrate on conservation.

It is extremely unlikely that more funds will be made available in the United Kingdom in the foreseeable future – whichever political party is in power – and the time to introduce positive tax-incentives (as opposed to current measures entailing the possibility of some small remission of Capital Transfer or Gains tax) similar to those offered by less philistine governments, is long overdue. Much of the richest material given to American universities over the years was the result of tax deduction incentives (subsequently rescinded) and the continuing success of official bodies such as the Archives of Ontario (part of the Canadian Ministry of Citizenship and Culture) is all the evidence (see previous chapter) anyone needs for the way to induce individuals to part with personal treasures, during their lifetime or after. The predicament of British colleges depending on voluntary contributions (which cannot be offset against tax) from 'Friends of the . . .', inviariably former students, is humiliating if they allowed themselves to think about it.

But some still manage to grow. It is not my intention to provide a league table of merit; comparisons are, in any case, impossible with so little common ground. At Oxford, for example, apart from the Bodleian – so privileged that it has enjoyed its copyright status, entitling it to a copy of every book published in the UK, for fifty years longer than any of the other four – some of the college libraries are quite small although collectively impressive. Cambridge too has an imposing tradition while other universities are outstanding in specialist and therefore narrower spheres. My very personal selection is made up of libraries who resist the temptation to rest on their laurels, whose sights are set on nothing less than excellence and who, particularly in the public sector, refuse to accept the restrictions imposed by inadequate funding.

When one considers that the establishment of the world's great libraries has taken hundreds of years, the most remarkable achievement of the twentieth century has been the rise in status of the Humanities Research Center at the University of Texas in Austin; in some respects a mirror image of the 'overnight' transformation of a backwater British colony into the world's most powerful nation. The feat is more significant than mind-boggling statistics – 9 million manuscripts, 800,000 rare books, 5 million photographs, possibly the world's largest collection of film/theatre memorabilia, and 50,000 items of literary iconography. In little more than a quarter of a century it has made Austin, the research capital of the world. Much has already been written about the HRC, but the scale of the operation is so vast and growing so steadily that one could spend years in the place and still find fresh interests.

The story began with Dr Harry Ransom (in 1983 the Center was renamed in his memory although it is easier to use the original initials), whose characteristic American dynamism generated such a powerful energy force that it might run forever on its own momentum. Indeed, having established the foundations for a great library, the Center subsequently decided it was no longer necessary to buy on such a lavish scale although, because of that momentum, the inflow of material has been maintained in the form of donations. But today, buying ranks third in priority behind conservation and cataloguing; by the end of the century as much as half of the total budget will be devoted to conservation.

Obviously, no institution of this calibre can operate without teams of dedicated and talented men and women, but to Ransom must go much of the credit for a project which to many men in his situation might have remained a dream in the realms of fantasy. The Center was established in 1957 after Ransom, the university administrator, had persuaded the governors to give him *carte blanche* with a first year budget of $2M (then approximately £800,000) a sum large enough to spread thickly. But far from 'spreading' his money, Ransom immediately invested *half* of it at the first opportunity – beating off rival universities and dealers for a unique collection of rare British modern first editions, manuscripts and letters so vast it had taken over the large house in which it was stored; the material filled every cupboard in every room and in every space – such as under the beds, as well as a large barn. It would have taken weeks to sort through everything, so Ransom bid for the lot uncatalogued, and it was only after they were eventually unpacked that the true value of his literary treasure could be appreciated. It was the sort of inspired gamble that distinguished the great collectors and book dealers from the ordinary.

From the outset, Ransom's incentive was the conviction that a university could not pretend to its title unless 'it contributes something to what all universities may teach in the future.' Enlarging on this philosopy, the present Director of the HRC, Mr Dechard Turner says: 'The Center exists to furnish the raw materials for the continued growth of scholarship. Its materials are like the fuel to a huge academic furnace that has to be constantly fed so that papers, articles, books and dissertations can be produced.'

Mr Turner explains: 'The Ransom revolution changed bibliographic geography. Reduced to one basic conclusion, it was that the first edition is not the beginning of the literary process, but rather its end . . . the end of a long and at times tortuous process consisting of the author's original notes; the manuscript; the corrected, rewritten (perhaps many times rewritten) manuscript; copy for printer; galley proofs; corrected galley proofs; page proofs; corrected page proofs, and ultimately the printed book*. In other words, the true seat of analysis, criticism and understanding of the literary process lies in the pre-published materials, and thus the need for complete archival collections.

It is clear now that Dr Ransom's central idea was an astonishing combination of foresight and necessity. Once he turned attention to the preliminary artefacts, it opened a fertile whole new world, and gave scholarship a massive area in which to work and come to a new understanding of the literary process. From the standpoint of

---

*Any novice collector reading this need not be alarmed. A number of these stages are skipped these days by publishers in the case of the majority of their authors; they are too conscious of budget considerations.

literary criticism, this was the greatest event of our time, for it released the author from the dominance of the first printed edition.'

It is easy to become preoccupied with modern works, and we have to remind ourselves that the Center's literary treasures cover every period. In 1986 it assumed curatorship of the Pforzheimer Library's collection of more than 1,100 volumes and approximately 250 groups of letters and documents spanning the period 1475–1700 – the last major collection representing the foundations of English culture remaining in private hands. Statistics related to the Center's acquisitions are invariably on such a large scale that they become almost meaningless, but when broken down we discover that this library – presented to the Center by Texas billionaire businessman, H. Ross Perot* includes among *eight* Caxtons, the first book printed in the English language, *Recuyell of the Historyes of Troye* (1475); the Shakespeare quartos and four folios of 1623, 1632, 1663 and 1685; the Coverdale Bible of 1535, the first complete bible in English; and we get a better perspective of its importance. The manuscripts are also impressive, including no less than six personal letters from Queen Elizabeth I.

The Center is particularly strong in nineteenth-century fiction, an extensive collection strengthened in 1983 by the English literature holdings of a Harvard professor, Robert Lee Wolff (7,000 entries representing 16,000 volumes), its desirability described by one authority as second only to the Gutenberg Bible (a copy of which was purchased in 1978 for $2.4M). The following year, a bequest from an Italian-born collector added 287 classical tracts printed between 1495 and 1588 in Venice by the incomparable Aldine Press begun by Aldus Manutius. Worth at least $2M, the collection is invaluable not only for some of the authors, but for its importance to the student of early printing and

---

*The larger-than-life philanthropic Mr Perot is better known for some of his more sensational activities, e.g. the hiring of commandos to rescue two of his employees held in Iran (recounted in Ken Follett's book *On Wings of Eagles*), and his financial backing of the abortive attempt to free the American hostages in Beirut in 1986. Earlier in that year, in Dallas, the Prince of Wales presented Mr Perot with the Winston Churchill Foundation award for displaying qualities reminiscent of the wartime leader.

binding. The Center is also very strong in French literature, housing probably the largest collection of books, manuscripts and letters outside France.

But in keeping with the University's tradition, almost everything is available for legitimate research and since this is the only place where one can find such in-depth material, it attracts not just those interested in the arts, but in the sciences – where else in the world could one find Einstein's original notes for the theory of relativity? (this among more than five hundred pages of unpublished notes written during the last five years of his life); the papers of the astronomer Sir William Herschel (1738–1822) and his son, Sir John; as well as the personalised ephemera of history, such as the billiard cue and spectacles of Sir Arthur Conan Doyle; the ball gown of Vivien Leigh (Scarlett O'Hara) from the film *Gone With The Wind*; the handcuffs (among many other possessions) of escapologist, Harry Houdini.

Items like this bring the past to life. The art of biography has been debased by the modern trend of settling for a paste and scissors job on published material. It is an unfortunate fact that the financial rewards of most exhaustively thorough biographers seldom adequately compensates them in terms of the time spent in research. If, like lawyers and similar professional people they charged for their time they would be rich men or women. The Center's collection of George Bernard Shaw material, finest in the world, is so comprehensive that it took Michael Holroyd seven weeks to complete that aspect of his research; nor did he neglect any of the other worthwhile collections of Shaw memorabilia. Not many biographers would be prepared to spend that amount of time on gathering raw material, but there is no reason why even 'mass-appeal' biography should not be properly researched. Who would not be fascinated by the private papers of the charismatic Lady Ottoline Morrell, which includes 7,760 items of correspondence?

On the impact of Dr Ransom's dream, Mr Turner says: 'His foresight enabled this institution to obtain vast literary treasures for pennies, a bit like getting Manhattan for a handful of beads. Such economic advantage did not last long. That which was at first laughed at quickly became one of the strongest collecting areas of the whole bibliographic field. As the Ransom Revolution opened a massive new sphere for academic involvement, the very same opening gave a new vitality and opportunity to booksellers.'

Conceding that this boom created its own drawbacks, Mr Turner points out: 'Bits and pieces and pre-publication review copies have come to command prices that are astronomical and foolish. Viewed at any other time in history, it would be judged an insanity to pay $575 for an unbound review copy, while the first edition in its published binding is available for $35. But this is mild. Consider the case of a third revised typescript with only two minor pencil changes being offered for $10,000 – and being sold. The first printed edition of the same text is widely available for $25. The only claim to importance is that the expensive items were from the pre-publication period. Such is testimony for the capacity of commerce to mutilate and inflate the best of ideas.'

Three well equipped conservation laboratories – for bindings, flat paper and photographs (see Chapter 7) – demonstrate the Center's stake in conservation – probably greater than in any other research library in the world, taking into consideration the diverse range of materials under risk. Referring to nineteenth- and twentieth-century literature, Dechard Turner says:

These come with built-in self-destruct quotients. Writers write on whatever is handy; wrapping paper, scraps of cardboard, yellow second sheets. And thus it is that the HRC collection of modern manuscripts, the largest literary legacy of its type in any one place in the world, faces a relatively quick destruction unless the inroads of deterioration are turned back.

The picture is made more complex in that the long neglected process of proper housing and care – a worldwide phenomenon – brings at the same time the need for binding conservation, photographic conservation, and *objets d'art* conservation. Conservation is a link in the chain of that ongoing educational enterprise represented by research libraries such as HRC.

The Humanities Research Center exists to furnish the raw materials for the continued growth of scholarship. Scholarship exists within a historic framework. The work of each generation must be available for comparison and correction. If the basic materials themselves fall into decay and disappear, the way is opened to the beginning of a new Dark Age. Chemistry and time have presented this generation of academic institutions a challenge: to keep the intellectual stride going, or let it slack into nonexistence.

Nor is the HRC interest in books confined to their content; its collection of fine bindings as part of a study of book history is superb and the section dealing with modern binding – especially post 1950 – is probably the best in the world. The work of British binders, as distinct from other Europeans and American craftsmen, is represented in terms of quality and quantity on a larger scale than the combined collections of libraries and museums in the UK.

Such is the scale of the whole operation – there are whole rooms set out as replicas of the studies or libraries of important authors or statesmen – that one wonders instinctively about the problems of space, until we remember that unlike national or copyright libraries where space has to be found for almost every book published in that country, universities can afford to be selective. Despite the common belief that, left to their own devices, books indulge in some reproductive process unknown to science, the supply of existing material available to reference libraries must inevitably diminish, so that the University of Texas, with four large buildings dominated by a purpose-built seven-storey limestone structure, should not have to resort to microfilm. However, thinking to the future, laser-beam storage is one possibility under consideration.

In view of its late start, Texas probably stands alone, but overhauling them in one area – that of contemporary writing and history – is the Twentieth Century Archives, part of the Special Collections department of the libraries of Boston University. Boston, for long in the shadow of Harvard, America's oldest university, has in the space of a few years risen in stature largely on the strength of this part of its library.

When the Archives were opened in 1963, a decision was taken to make their own judgements on the quality of the work and papers of the individuals to be collected; not to wait for Time's seal of approval. In this way the Library was able not only to stake its claims ahead of its rivals, but also pay (if this was necessary) far less than the eventual market price. As a result, the work of almost all modern writers of merit has been and continues to be solicited – in many cases before that talent is generally recognised.

The policy is commendably bold, although one wonders whether in fifty years or so, with the inevitable pressures on space, a number of writers who do not fulfill their promise will not be jettisoned. The library is naturally reticent about this prospect, but apprehension is based on the very *raison d'etre* of the Archives, which is 'to reflect the many aspects of contemporary life', and such a collection cannot remain open-ended. Over a thousand individual 'files' already in existence are not restricted to authors but include poets, playwrights, critics, journalists, cartoonists, actors, directors, producers and musicians; those outside the arts are diplomats, statesmen, military and civil rights leaders, and others in public life.

One would not be surprised that American public affairs are well documented, yet the scale is quite daunting, e.g. there are *four million* documents covering the long political career of Speaker of the House of Representatives, John W. McCormack, spanning the presidencies of Calvin Coolidge and Richard Nixon. Yet one might ask why it is Boston and not a British university which holds the papers not only of Cecil King, the press baron who built the Mirror newspapers group (it is not so long ago that the Daily Mirror was Britain's outstanding popular newspaper), but those of his uncles, Viscounts Northcliffe and Rothermere, pioneers of modern British journalism. Family diaries, journals, correspondence and documents dating from the eighteenth century, provide an invaluable fund of research for the study of newspapers and journalism. It is typical, in my opinion, of the foresight of American librarians, which inspired Howard Gotlieb, director of the Archives to recognise the academic value of such a collection before any British institution and then write to Cecil King to ask if the papers might be deposited at Boston. I suspect that the conscious interest of a number of British universities ends with the nineteenth century; of the others, too many lack the initiative to do anything other than wait for such items to come up at auction – where, in any case, they probably could not afford to compete. The admirable British Library of Political and Economic Science (i.e. The London School of Economics) is an exception, housing as it does important G. B. Shaw material, such as his business papers, but the breadth of its coverage of 'ordinary' requirements (it has over two million books) has become a millstone. But too many others are apathetic. I have a friend in London whose growing collection of modern literature may one day be offered to a college or university; the irony is that the onus will be on him to find a deserving library prepared to accept it.

No accurate account of the century could be written without access to the papers of men and women who fashioned it – the principal actors on a world stage which, with the birth and development of movements like Civil Rights, has presented dramas of far greater magnitude than anything created in the mind of a playwright. Here is the handwritten manuscript with alterations of Martin Luther King's sermon 'Shattered Dreams' (among 83,000 documents in the Dr King 'file'), far more evocative than the final text, revealing more of the man's character. Similarly, the researcher can find Alistair Cooke's eye-witness report – the scrawled and amended notes – on the assassination of Robert Kennedy in 1968.

The literary content of the Archives is enormous, but addicts of the mystery and suspense novel would be particularly fascinated by the wealth of original material in this field, so long neglected as a literary form. The large group of writers represented provide an engrossing illustration through much pre-published material of the way art has transformed a neglected genre. Housed here are all the elements of the writer's craft – manuscripts, notes and notebooks and memorabilia – representing such diverse styles and talents as Eric Ambler, distinguished film writer as well as novelist, Leslie Charteris creator of *The Saint*, Robert van Gulik, Ngaio Marsh, and Mignon Eberhart, among many favourites. Indeed, if ever a collection merited a 'seal of approval', it was bestowed in 1976 when the Mystery Writers of America placed its own comprehensive library of first editions, page and galley proofs on deposit at Boston.

Although my main interest was in the Twentieth Century Archives, it is impossible to leave Boston without brief reference to another of the special collections, the History of Nursing Archives, established in 1966, obviously fascinating in its own right, but of special interest to English historians if only for its collection of material relating to Florence Nightingale, founder of modern nursing. Influenced by the romantic image of the 'lady with the lamp', most people see Florence Nightingale as a symbol of gentleness and compassion, forgetting how much more significant was her role as a pioneer of modern medical practice and post operative care. The first editions of her books in this collection include *A Contribution to the Sanitary History of the British Army During the Late War with Russia*, published anonymously in 1859, and a sixpenny edition of *Notes on Nursing for the Labouring Classes*, signed by the author and with a letter dated September 1869 – just one in a collection of 175 letters dating from 1851 to 1900 on a variety of serious topics, including sanitation in India. Several of the letters written from the Scuteri Barrack hospital, included one (27 January, 1856) to General Sir Howard Douglas about a savings bank system for the soldiers in the Crimea.

The problems of the United Kingdom's five designated copyright deposit libraries – to which some 70,000 entries annually may be added to existing catalogues (in itself another conservation headache) are greater than most. I suspect those of the British Library, with limitless parameters, are virtually insurmountable, outside Government intervention in the form of tax incentives on gifts, or even the introduction of state lotteries. The essential pressures of 'below the line' expenditure (overheads, conservation etc) on the total budget inevitably reduces the funds for buying which then have to be split between the justifiable but conflicting demands of different departments. When I was researching *Fine Bookbinding in the Twentieth Century* (David & Charles 1984), I expressed surprise at the inadequacy of their representative coverage of recent British bindings – to be informed that the bindings budget allocation covered all periods, and that the sudden availability of an interesting collection (e.g. the work of seventeenth century French craftsmen), might swallow the total budget for that year – the justification being that the old volumes may never appear again, whereas young binders will continue to produce interesting work. That is true, but unfortunately the best time to buy any art form is before the artist/craftsman has made his/her mark – which is why so many outstanding examples of modern binding are today housed at the HRC in Austin and other American universities, purchased at a time when most British institutions were still saying of the binder 'Who?'

When a library's terms of reference are more clearly defined, the problems are reduced proportionately. The National Library of Scotland comes into this category, but I have singled it out partly because of the energetic way it interprets its function; even more for its positive approach to situations that would daunt most others.

The first time I took any serious notice of this library was early in 1986 when it succeeded in raising $920,000 for the purchase from the United States of two important collections of manuscripts of Sir Walter Scott. For years there have been moans about the loss of so much British heritage to marauding American libraries and museums. Why, it has been asked, should we have to go to Texas to research 'our' D. H. Lawrence, conveniently ignoring similar complaints from Greeks who have to catch a plane to London to see the Elgin Marbles.

In civilised society, literary and art treasures should go to the most appreciative homes, and the Scott collections were received by the National Library of Scotland because they were important enough to demand a special effort at a time when the money was simply not available. Admittedly, their cause was assisted by sympathetic vendors who might have realised more by sale on the open market, but then fortune favours the brave.

A little background information at this stage will help put this and future purchases into context. The National Library is a successor to the Advocates Library founded in the late seventeenth century, inheriting its collection of books and manuscripts (with the exception of those appertaining to law, to which it still has full access). In 1710, by an Act of Parliament of Queen Anne entitled 'For the Encouragement of Learning', it obtained the right of copyright deposit, which it has retained to the present day. During the eighteenth century, the facilities of the library were used more widely and one of the keepers, David Hume, initiated a policy of buying the best works of Continental (especially French) scholarship, culminating in the purchase of two great collections; the library of the Icelandic scholar, Grimur Thorkelin, with its Icelandic and Scandinavian books and manuscripts – Scotland has usually enjoyed closer ties than England with Scandinavia and France – and the Spanish library of the Astorga family.

The library was growing all the time in quality as well as size; its

115

third printed catalogue, published in six volumes and a supplement between 1867 to 1879, containing 260,000 entries. With the gift of £100,000 by Sir Alexander Grant of Forres as an endowment (to be repeated with a similar sun towards the construction of a new building), the Government in 1925 accepted the Faculty's offer to present the library to the nation. The official change in status stimulated a further series of notable gifts of books and manuscripts.

In 1974, the Scottish Central Library, responsible for inter-library loans, merged with the National Library which assumed its responsibilities. Today, the library houses three million printed books – needless to say, the largest number of Scottish books to be found in one library – beginning with the only surviving copies of the earliest examples of Scottish printing, the nine tracts printed by Walter Chepman and Andro Myllar at Edinburgh in 1508. Foreign books include its greatest single treasure, an illuminated copy of the Gutenberg Bible.

It is the Department of Manuscripts with which we are concerned in relation to the spectacular Scott purchases (and the no less remarkable follow-up in 1986, the raising of £550,000/$797,500 to buy the Murthly Book of Hours, an illuminated manuscript of around 1310, and as such the oldest 'book' associated with Scotland) has an equally impressive history in its own right. In both cases money continued to pour in to the Department long after the closing dates, so that they were able to hand back a fair surplus to one of their staunchest supporters, the National Heritage Memorial Fund.

The first manuscripts received by the original Advocates Library were legal documents such as (in 1683) an early copy of the Regiam Majestatem, early code of the laws of Scotland, but three years later the gift of a thirteenth century Gratian (the Italian monk recognised as founder of the science of canon law), began to widen the library's range. Over the years the Faculty expanded its collection of manuscripts with a will and, as early as 1700 it was evident that it was not content to merely receive or purchase manuscripts brought to its attention. A leaflet issued at that time stated principles of acquisition which read today as an early precedent for the Scott and Murthly Hours coups:

There being many *Manuscripts* and *Monuments of Antiquity*, in the Hands of several Persons, or in the Charter Chests of Ancient Families, which, if still keep't Latent, will be Useless to the Publick, and expos'd to many Accidents, that are prevented by their lying in a publick *Library*. Therefore it is earnestly desired, That the Havers of any such, whether *Histories*, *Chartularies of Monastries*, *Old Charters*, or other *Manuscripts* whatsoever, would be pleas'd to send them in to the *Advocates Library*; where such Benefactors, and their Donatives, shall be Faithfully Recorded, and Honourable Mention also made of Them, in publick *Catalogues*, to be printed by the *Faculty*.

All other persons likewise, who are possessors of, and who design to Sell, any such *Manuscripts*, are also Invited to bring them in; And the *Curators* of the said *Library* will Pay them therefore, to their Satisfaction.

Because of the emotional aspect of the Scott campaign, many people lost sight of the fact that there were two separate collections at stake. The first, offered by the Pforzheimer Library in New York, although important for the light it throws on different periods of Sir Walter Scott's writing, was inevitably overshadowed by the magnitude of the second, secured from Dartmouth College, New Hampshire. The Pforzheimer collection, the manuscripts of three novels and one major poem* (together with some lesser material) were added to the library's existing manuscripts, as well as many thousand letters – the largest collection of Scott letters in

---

*For most of us, Scott's success as a writer of historical fiction – the first and (some say) the greatest – has obscured his prowess as a poet. Indeed, Scott considered himself a poet and turned to prose writing only after establishing his reputation, during which period, he could have become the Poet Laureate, declining the honour in favour of Southey. His first novel, *Waverley*, was published anonymously in 1814, the identity of the author of this and subsequent works in the genre, remaining a secret for ten years. Although the novels were an instant success, Scott's lifestyle (apart from the costs of his estate, his hugely lavish entertaining included bringing King George IV to Edinburgh) necessitated a constant output. Even so, he managed to keep his head above water until 1826 when the publishing firm in which he was a partner collapsed with debts of a quarter of a million pounds, an enormous sum in those days. As though inspired by one of his fictitious heroes, Scott took it upon himself to repay this debt – by the only way he knew how – 'this right hand shall work it off,' he declared.

the world. (Pforzheimer is, of course, one of the great libraries and this relatively small sale, coinciding with the massive collection bought by Mr Ross Perot for the HRC of Texas signalled a change of policy whereby certain sections of the library were sold in order to strengthen other collections, e.g. the English Romantics (Shelley etc).

However, the other collection known as the Magnum Opus, forty-one unique volumes of the Waverley novels, is especially fascinating because of the circumstances in which they were compiled. In 1823, his publisher Archibald Constable, anticipating the author's guaranteed place in literary history, as well as another publishing coup, suggested that consideration be given to the compilation of a special definitive record of his works. He wrote:

> It need not be disguised that there has been nothing produced in the Literary World at any period about which there will be hereafter so much said, written and published as the Works of the Author of Waverley. There will be attempts at illustrations and notes of all sorts, kinds and designations, full of absurdities and blunders; and in my opinion it is the Author only who could do anything at all acceptable in the way of genuine illustration. . . . I would respectfully submit this to you as a project for consideration, and if you will permit me I shall have a set of all the Tales, Novels and Romances interleaved and neatly done up to be placed in a suitable cabinet in your private study . . .

Into these forty-one interleaved volumes made up by him and his successor, Robert Cadell (kinsman of the library's current Keeper of Manuscripts), Scott made additions, alterations and corrections. He added long historical notes and introductory matter, all subsequently bound in. This work of considerable scholarship was compiled during the most harrowing years of his life, writing day and night to pay off his debts, being almost complete by the time of his death in 1832; some of it being included in the popular Magnum edition published between 1929–33. The original *Magnus Opus* (Scott's own title) which turned up many years later in the United States, was described in the brochure prepared to spearhead the fund-raising compaign, as:

. . . unquestionably the most outstanding Scottish literary treasure in private hands. It represents the Wizard of the North's last thoughts on his own greatest works of imagination. . . . Perhaps the ultimate 'association copy', for its sentimental and emotional value is incalculable. It is the greatest monument of one of the immortal episodes in literary history. In its thousands of pages of annotations and additions in his own hand, one can see Sir Walter Scott struggling valiantly hour by hour, day in, day out, to pay off his crippling debts by the exercise of his prodigious talents as historian and story-teller in a labour which is unparalleled in the annals of literature.

Another direct benefit of the acquisition, anticipated by the library, was its value in the preparation of the forthcoming definitive 'Edinburgh' edition of the Waverley novels, which are likely to be published between 1990 and the end of the century. Because of Scott's desire to keep his identity secret, the manuscripts were transcribed before printing, increasing the risk of error in the final text – a problem apparently accentuated by the fact that he was not too hot as a proof reader (few authors are, tending to read what they imagine should be there and not what is actually in print). The new edition will be an attempt to get back to what the author (with the help of the 'new' notes) originally intended. It is also proposed to provide critical introductions and notes. As a publishing event it should surpass the achievement of the updated editions of the Pepys *Diaries* in the 1970s, not only in context, but in the amount of original material presented.

Even before the library trustees were toasting their success with the Scott material, it was responding to an offer from Sotheby's negotiating the sale of the Murthly Book of Hours on behalf of the Marquess of Bute. They asked for and were given six months to raise the asking price of £550,000 before the manuscript was put on the market. As the name suggests, the Book of Hours was a volume of private prayers and devotions, consisting of a total of 215 leaves. It is written in a fine Gothic liturgical hand, with illuminated initials for every verse and line 'fillers' of coloured flowers, dragons, animals etc on burnished gold, as well as borders formed of weird figures, dragons, and groups of monks, and kings. It has eleven very large initials containing scenes from the life of Christ;

in addition there are twenty-three full-page miniatures.

The identity of the person for whom it was made is not known but it is believed to have been in Scotland in about 1420, when it was in the possession of the Stewarts, Lords of Lorne. It remained with different branches of the family until it was sold in 1871 by the Stewarts of Murthly. Apart from its value as a remarkable work of art – it was the finest medieval manuscript in private hands in Scotland – the Gaelic charm on one of the fly-leaves dates from the fourteenth century and thought to be the oldest example of the written use of that language. How it came to be added to a manuscript written in Latin is not clear, but Patrick Cadell, Keeper of Manuscripts, suggests it may have been inserted by the first owner or added in the sixteenth century when the book was re-bound. 'The practice of associating a charm with a religious text is known,' he says, 'as contagious magic – or, more mundanely, as hedging one's bets!'

But fourteenth-century manuscripts are hardly run-of-the-mill and attract attention that could obscure the excellent work going on in other areas. To me, perhaps the most interesting activity at the National Library is the steady, unheralded gathering of the works and papers of modern Scottish writers, reflecting the creative talent established, and as yet little known, of that nation. The Department of Manuscripts has an impressive record in this field, but its current policy of not waiting for writers to become international celebrities – similar in philosophy to that of the University of Boston – must inevitably pay off, even though some material may not stand the test of time.

The department has attempted to build up a collection more widely based than just working drafts and notebooks, to include correspondence and personal papers. Correspondence tends to throw more light than creative works do upon what a particular writer was thinking, and upon the individuals and ideas by which he or she was influenced. The relative smallness of the Scottish literary renaissance makes the acquisition of their often interlocking correspondence particularly useful. There have been a number of very talented Scottish writers since Burns, Scott and Stevenson, and whether the reputations of the current crop survive for as long remains to be seen – although some such as J. M. Barrie and John Buchan have already made their marks. Among the many important papers housed here are those of personal favourites, Neil Gunn, George Mackay Brown and Naomi Mitchison.

As an extension of this programme they also acquire the papers of artists and musicians, printers and publishers, considered important for completing the cultural picture.

The assumption that the quality of great writing transcends national boundaries is not as obvious as it might seem; the work of some authors and playwrights does not necessarily survive translation. There are a number of reasons; not just the complexities of dialect – indeed, it has been said that the works of Robert Burns are more widely known in Russia than they are in England. But interest in George Bernard Shaw, for example, remains truly international; he has been translated not only into Russian but Arabic, among a variety of languages.

Because of the breadth of Shaw's talent, and the fact that he was ninety-four when he died in 1950, it would be virtually impossible to collate such a massive output of pre-published and pre-production material, papers and memorabilia. In addition to the largest single collection at the HRC in Austin, there are substantial holdings at Cornell University in New York State, and Boston's Twentieth Century Archives – quite apart from impressive holdings at the British Library – yet another (the largest still remaining in private hands) turned up in 1986 at the Canadian University of Guelph. One is hard put not to sound patronising – who and where is Guelph? Even Canadians who have heard of the place (the nearest major city is Toronto) know it only for the traditional excellence of its schools of agriculture and veterinary medicine. (In 1974 the original Ontario Agricultural College celebrated its one hundreth anniversary.) All that is changing fast.

Admittedly, Guelph did not go looking for the Shaw material (although its library merits inclusion in this chapter for the numbers and quality of its books on Scotland – probably the largest outside that country) but they were not found wanting when the opportunity arose. The collection was obtained from Professor Dan Laurence, leading American Shaw scholar, being the playwright's authorised bibliographer and editor of his collected letters. The material amassed over years by the professor included not only original manuscripts and playscripts (rehearsal copies having Shaw's characteristic textual alterations scribbled in the margins), but all known recordings of Shaw's voice, costume design sketches made by the author in 1894, for a production of *Arms and the Man,* and the only known surviving copy of an essay on pornography entitled *Flagellomania,* published (in English) in France in 1899, in which GBS gives his view on whipping.

Guelph was chosen because Professor Laurence has a special affection for Ontario – he taught at the University during one visit in 1984, and is literary advisor to the Shaw Festival – the theatre at Niagara Falls being the only one in the world devoted to the playwright's work. It is no coincidence that the University houses the Festival's archives, which it began acquiring in the mid-1970s. The $10,000 it had to find for the Laurence material is only a fraction of the market value, which is probably ten times that amount. That is, admittedly, because of its unusual nature. 'Ordinary' Shaw first editions, particularly of his later works, are not in great demand, although in common with most 'cycles' no doubt that will change in due course.

Today's purpose-built six-floor library is light years away from the humble set-up of a hundred years ago. At the Ontario Agricultural College, students were entitled to borrow books, if they could overcome the obstacles placed in their way! In 1881 rules and regulations stipulated that 'books may be obtained or exchanged any day (Sundays excepted) between 1 and 2 o'clock p.m. No student is allowed to have more than one book from the Library at the same time. No person shall retain a book longer than one week . . .' The term 'library' was somewhat grandiose at the time, not meriting a building of its own until 1903, when the Massey Hall and Library was designed to hold 75,000 volumes. That was quite ambitious because the College's collection at the time only totalled 11,000. In due course other collections sprang up on various locations on campus, but it was not until 1965 when the college became a university, with much broader interests, that certain people began to see the potential for a major library.

The scope of the growth programme for the new library, completed in 1968, is reflected in the flexible modular design which incorporates stacks on each floor interspaced with complementary study and service areas, and everything interchangeable with minimum effort. It meant that with an *ultimate* capacity of three-quarters-of-a-million volumes, it had already passed the one million mark within ten years, while at the twenty year mark, the figures will have reached two million. Although material related to agriculture initially accounted for a significant part of the present library, a stream of fine 'new' collections has steadily broadened its range, so that it compares today with the top university libraries.

The size of the Scottish and Scottish-Canadian collections is even more remarkable because unlike those of the longstanding agriculture and veterinary interests, it was only started when the university was established. The reason for its accelerated growth was an interest that straddled the individual claims of different academic departments. It was fuelled by a sense of pride in the history of a relatively young nation, and the fact that a large number of Canadians have Scottish ancestry. The goal was assisted by the formation of an Interdepartmental Committee on Scottish studies responsible for graduate programmes on masters' and doctorate levels which meant that in addition to normal library funds, Guelph has been able to secure grants over a wider field from private and government sources. Today the Scottish collection is strong across the board, but highlights include mini-collections within the overall framework, such as manuscripts, the Jacobite period, Burgh records, Government documents and Church history, pamphlets and broadsides.

It is a fact that the more active a library, the more it attracts donations and bequests from scholars and collectors. Some of these were to be expected, such as a large collection of the works and papers of John Galt, the distinguished nineteenth century novelist, playwright – who founded the town of Guelph! Another interesting literary cache is that of L. M. Montgomery, which includes her papers and personal diaries spanning 1889 to 1942 and running to over two million words. Less so, but certainly not out-of-place are political themes with an international flavour, such as a collection of Soviet World War II posters, or in-depth studies of narrow subjects such as witchcraft, and a huge library on apiculture.

Six

THE DUST JACKET

There is nothing like demand and inflated prices to concentrate the attention, and in recent years everyone has become dust jacket conscious, recognising the fact that a modern first edition without a fine wrapper is as incomplete as breakfast cereal without milk . . . but that is about all we do know.

Most of us are embarrassingly ignorant about this 'new' facet of collecting, and a bibliographical study is much overdue; although, unfortunately, because of the lack of available information, the necessary research would take years. Meanwhile, myths and repeated inaccuracies die hard. I once made the mistake of asking an ostensibly experienced bookseller (at least, he'd been in the trade for over half a century) what he knew about dust jackets. 'You mean dust *wrappers!*', he said. On reflection, giving him the benefit of the doubt, his smile might have been courteous as much as patronising, but at the time I felt suitably chastened by someone who ought to have known. Innocently, I questioned his authority for that assertion, asking the source of his information. This time he blustered a little, muttering something about it being a 'fact', and that the term 'jacket' being an unfortunate 'Americanism'.

One of the first things one learns in the book-world is that experience should – but does not necessarily equal knowledge. Some people learn more in five years than others in fifty; it is a question of being interested in extending one's horizons, and if a person is not bothered, then the 'experience' adds up to 10% knowledge, and 90% revision. The problem in this context is that for many years even distinguished bibliographers totally and quite deliberately ignored the existence of book jackets, and since collectors invariably threw them away, it hardly mattered. In relation to the history of books, dust jackets are almost an 'overnight' phenonemon. No one but a crank started collecting them until the 1920s (slightly earlier in the United States), and interest did not develop until the 1930s – mainly as a result of collector's correspondence in *Publishers Weekly*. The first exhibition of jackets was not until 1945, organised at the Victoria and Albert Museum by Charles Rosner, one of only a handful of experts on the subject.

So it is not all that surprising that there remains a certain inconsistency in talk of wrappers or jackets. Yet in a paper 'Book-Jackets, Blurbs and Bibliographers', given to the American Bibliographical Society in 1970, G. Thomas Tanselle, American collector and one of the few authorities in this very special field, should have ended the ambiguity. With supporting evidence, he pointed out that the term 'wrapper' referred to a paper cover which is physically attached to the sheets it covers, whereas 'jacket' has been in use at least since the 1890s in the context of a *detachable* paper covering for a book.

So if that very positive explanation is an 'Americanism', then so be it! Despite the tendency of a few diehard Europeans to regard the United States as some primitive backwoods, it must be said that the history of dust jackets in our two countries is comparable, and in advance of those on the Continent. Despite the huge gaps in our knowledge, it is reasonable to conclude that in the United States from the 1880s, 80% of books published were issued with dust jackets – more than in the United Kingdom. Yet it was not a race in any sense, and credit must go to the handful of innovative publishers on both sides of the Atlantic who recognised the potential value of this additional display area, with the use of colour and design.

Material appertaining to the origins of the 'modern' jacket is very sparse. There are only two* thin English language books written on the subject, and a couple of decent 'bibliographies'† and

*Rosner (Charles), *The Growth of the Dust Jacket*, Sylvan Press 1954
 Weidemann (Kurt), *Book Jackets & Record Covers*: an International Survey 1969
†Tanselle (G. Thomas), *Book Jackets, Blurbs and Bibliographers*, The Library (USA) June 1971
 Sale Catalogue of the Ken Leach Collection of nineteenth century American Books in Original Dust Jackets and Boxes (June 1984), Oinonen Book Auctions, MA 01375, USA.

my own superficial research almost immediately found likely errors of fact; new early jackets are constantly coming to light. What we do know is that they were introduced in the nineteenth century, but records are uneven because the initial concept was to merely provide a means of protecting cloth binding from dust and marks in transit from publisher to bookshop, and subsequently in the customer's home; as such jackets had a built-in self-destruct quotient. They were not meant to survive constant handling and, in any case, were discarded by fastidious collectors, and almost all libraries, until quite recently (many lending libraries still throw them away, whether or not they have other means of protection). More significant is the fact that there is little available evidence of their history, outside the libraries of a handful of collectors. Apart from a few individual books which happen to have their original jacket, the major reference libraries have almost nothing to show – even the British Library has no jackets category of exhibit in the printed books or prints and manuscripts departments. (The notable exception, you will not be surprised to learn, is the HRC of the University of Texas!)

There are, of course, a few exhibits spread very thinly, such as at the Victoria and Albert Museum where the depth of their interests in art in its various forms means that there is a small collection of jackets designed by artists in the 1920s and 1930s. There is nothing really old, but I was intrigued to find an engraving for a design on a 'wrapper' for a book on gold leaf, published in the *eighteenth* century, considerably in advance of the first recorded jackets. Immediately preceding the 'modern' jacket publishers had sometimes used 'envelopes' or sleeves, which completely enclosed a book, or boxes (a device which is still used to protect fine bindings), but as to what form this wrapping took cannot even be speculated since the exhibit is very small and no other information is available; nor is the quality of the design good enough to reproduce here so you are not even able to make an inspired guess!

Ironically, since rarity is so directly linked to values, there is relatively little interest in early dust jackets. The book, for whatever reason, is always the collectors' main target – the jacket in later years becoming an essential part of the whole (although seldom bought and sold on their own) – so that jackets for early Ian Fleming titles are worth considerably more than one offered for its historical or rarity interest, adding hundreds of pounds to the value of the book. The exceptions would be limited to nineteenth century first editions which are themselves exceptionally rare and sought by collectors. To the best of my knowledge, nobody has yet turned up a first edition of *Dracula* (1897) complete with dust jacket; if they have, it has been kept very secret. The title is in demand even without one, so the price a 're-united' copy would fetch is anyone's guess – certainly not less than £3,000–£5,000, which is considerably more than (say) *Casino Royale*; but that, of course, would be very much a 'one-off'.

The reference books tell us that the earliest dust jackets in the United States date from 1829, compared with 1833 in England, and almost half a century later in France and Germany. I am indebted to the bookseller from Vermont, Ken Leach, a leading authority on nineteenth-century jackets, for pointing out that the very earliest were not what we regard as jackets (detachable paper covers) but labelled slipcases. During the period 1825–9, in both England and America, annuals such as the *Atlantic Souvenir*; *Forget-me-not*; *Juvenile Depository*, and *The Pledge of Friendship*, were issued in glazed boards usually green or blue, and came in cardboard slipcases, open at the top, with glazed printed labels.

Very little visible evidence remains of the first, now conventional jackets. The first British publisher to take this course was Longman in 1832 (issued 1833) with *Keepsake,* a rather sober affair of yellowish buff paper, although the ink used was red, giving the text some lift. On the front was the title in bold lettering, followed by a one-line description, and at the bottom the publisher's imprint; on the back a ruled panel containing an advertisement for three of Longman's books in the 'Works on the Fine Arts' series – a logical innovation that was ignored by most publishers who preferred to leave the space blank; in fact, some were content, presumably to save on printing costs, to merely give the title and nothing else. This jacket was once in the collection of John Carter, the distinguished bibliographer and author of (among others) *Taste & Technique in Book Collecting,* best remembered for the way he and Graham Pollard exposed the forgeries of Thomas Wise. (It is interesting that when Carter became President of the Bibliographical Society of America in 1969, he was following in the footsteps of the man he had helped unmask who had occupied that position in 1922.) However, today the only record of its existence is in a photograph which appeared in the two reference books mentioned, because it 'disappeared' on its way to the Bodleian Library in 1952.

Longman remained at the forefront (along with T. Fisher, also of London) in making good use of jacket space; in 1860 their illustrated edition of Bunyan's *Pilgrims Progress* was printed with the title lettering on a scroll design, and a large woodcut from the book on the front.

In 1844, Fisher introduced what was probably only the second dust jacket for a popular series of annual, *The Juvenile Scrapbook* (now in the University of California Library, Los Angeles). Like *The Keepsake* it was designed to enclose the book completely, although detachable. Print was confined to a ruled box yet quite eye-catching with, at the top, in capital letters the promotional headline: WITH SIXTEEN HIGHLY FINISHED PLATES. Presumably, because Fisher had an office in Paris, part of the title was also printed at the top in French: L'ALBUM DES ENFANTS followed by brief information, then repeated in English:

'Elegantly bound: Price Eight Shillings'

then the title in large bold type, and just below:

by The Author of
'THE WOMEN OF ENGLAND'
1845

and finally the publisher's imprint. (In the following year, the-editor, Mrs Sarah Ellis, was named on the jacket front.)

The move towards protecting covers was beginning to snowball, and two future best sellers – *Tom Brown's Schooldays* (illustrated edition) and *Hunting of the Snark* – were produced by Macmillan in London in 1869 and 1876 respectively. The later book, printed on front, back *and* spine, carried advertising for the two *Alice* titles, and also French, German and Italian translations of *Wonderland*.

Reference to other European countries reminds us that in France and Germany jackets did not appear until the 1890s, and never really caught on in the same way although both recognised the potential aesthetic appeal, and were ahead of us in using the talents of professional artists. Toulouse Lautrec was among several poster artists to produce jacket illustrations, one of his most striking being *Histoires Naturelles*, Paris 1899. In England and the United States artists were not actually commissioned until the 1920s. The English publisher, T. Fisher Unwin, is credited with being the first to consciously use a professionally designed decoration in 1906 when they produced an art-paper dust jacket with a three-colour design by Aubrey Beardsley for *The Dream and the Business*, by John Oliver Hobbes. However, it was not commissioned as such; the design, featuring a girl in a bookshop setting, had been purchased thirteen years earlier in the form of an advertising poster. But even this credit has been diluted in recent years when it was pointed out that Beardsley's work had been the inspiration of the binder, and the design on the jacket was simply a copy of that.

Meanwhile, the first recorded dust jacket in the United States – purchased with its book in 1922 by the Huntington Library in San Marino, California, where it is now housed – was *Poems*, by W. W. Lord, 1845, an attractively ambitious design. But this is disputed by Ken Leach, who maintains that he had, and sold, the earliest, entitled: Six Illustrations of *Rip Van Winkle*, no author, an oblong folio-size book published for Members of the American Art Union, 1848. The publication contains six mounted India-proof plates designed and etched by F. O. C. Darley, and the jacket is printed on front with a design and text different from anything in the book. Leach claims that *Poems* is a 'hybrid'; not a jacket by design, and suggests that it is a pamphlet with wrappers strengthened with cardboard, disqualifying it as a dust jacket. His theory is supported in part by Tanselle's 1970 paper, although now it is virtually impossible to be sure because soon after it was purchased by the Huntington Library, it was incorporated into the binding.

Keeping pace with the gathering momentum, American publishers were quick to capitalise on the opportunities for illustration, and in the 1880s a number of prominent artists were featured on dust jackets – probably the most attractively eye-catching to date being Frederick Remington's symbolic 'Wild West' design for *Ranch Life & the Hunting Trail*, by Theodore Roosevelt, produced by the Century Publishing Company, New York in 1888. By now, in the historical sense, it was becoming a succession of 'firsts'. In the useful catalogue to the sale of Ken

Leach's collection, for example, one finds what he believed to be the first known book published in California to appear with a dust jacket (*California Notes*, 1876, grey paper printed in black); arguably the first use of colour on an American jacket (*The Flood of Years*, 1878, printed in red); the first publisher's blurb (*Our Village*, 1880).

Although now assimilated into the language like so many slang expressions, the origins of the word 'blurb' are obscure. But if we take it to mean a form of editorial promotion as opposed to advertising copy, its use on dust jackets dates from that 1880 book, although still used only sparingly throughout the rest of the century. This may be why it is often believed that blurbs did not come into fashion until 1910; the misconception is probably due to the fact that the expression was not actually coined until 1907 when at an American booksellers' convention, the publisher B. W. Huebsch, endeavouring to promote the book, *Are You A Bromide?*, distributed 500 copies with a startling dust jacket (now in the Library of Congress) with just title and author (Gelett Burgess) in front centre, and the rest a blurb. At the top it read:

YES, this is a 'BLURB'!
All the Other Publishers commit them. Why Shouldn't We?

(In between was the representation of a young woman cupping a hand to her mouth, as though in the act of calling,) and the words on either side:

Miss Belinda Blurb   In the Act of Blurbing

Immediately below is the book's title and author, followed by the blurb:

Say? Aint this book a 90H.P., six-cylinder Seller? If WE do say it as shouldn't, WE consider that this man Burgess has got Henry James locked into the coal-bin, telephoning for 'Information' WE expect to sell 350 copies of this great, grand book. It has gush and go to it, it has that Certain Something which makes you want to crawl through thirty miles of dense tropical jungle and bite somebody in the neck. No hero or heroine, nothing like that for OURS, but when you've READ this masterpiece, you'll know what a BOOK is, and you'll sic it onto your mother-in-law, your dentist and the pale youth who dips hot air into Little

Majorie until 4A.M. in the front parlour. This book has 42 carat THRILLS IN IT. It fairly BURBLES. Ask the man at the counter what HE thinks of it! He's seen Janice Meredith faded into a mauve magenta. He's seen BLURBS before, and he's dead wise, He'll say:

This Book is the Proud Purple Penultimate!!

The humour is somewhat dated, but full marks for originality, and for the small panel on the flap headed: NOTICE: How To Read A Book. 'Lie on your back, on a table or smooth surface. Place your feet on the chandelier, then, holding the Book in one hand, look it over with the other. Begin at the Back, cursing the pictures gently. This should be done two or three times. Never buy a book when you can look it over and suck its blood from the booksellers, or get it from the library. It is liable to make the Author and the Bookseller too conceited and Affluent.'

But, as I said earlier, interest in early dust jackets is still sporadic. Ken Leach started his collection on a whim because he is fascinated by all unrecorded material. He began pulling older jackets from his stock of ordinary books, and one thing led to another. When he had assembled over 600 jacketed books up to the year 1900 he decided it was time to sell, partly to fund his other book buying activities. Initially he offered them as a collection to university libraries he assumed would be interested in an opportunity to acquire such a huge chunk of book history in one go. The price tag was modest – $25,000 – but it wasn't the cost which killed interest; it was the theme. No doubt, if he had the time and inclination to split the books up into individual lots and offer them individually to State libraries on the strength of the books alone, he would have found more enthusiasm – but no one was interested in dust jackets as a main attraction.

Because there was no point in selling some and keeping others, no reserve price was fixed, and consequently lots which did not sell were added to the next until a buyer was found; it meant that sometimes half a dozen would be knocked down for a few dollars. In the end the sale made a small profit, but the lesson – particularly in the case of something of antiquity – is that if there is no apparent interest, then leave it to try again at some future date; advice which is constantly demonstrated in antiques, for example, where periods go in and out of fashion.

Old jackets which are not falling to pieces can only appreciate in value, although within limits. I mentioned *Dracula* as an extreme example, but dust jackets do not necessarily add much to the value of a desirable book. You may have noticed the way some booksellers put inflated prices on a book they are in no hurry to sell because of its assured appreciation, and the same applies to jackets. At a Boston book fair, one of the stands had a copy of the famous *Oregon Trail*, 1892, with a practical dust jacket by Frederic Remington, priced at $1,200. I don't know if it sold on that occasion, but I do know that Ken Leach had a copy at about the same time, advertised extensively for $350 – but no sale.

Apart from the bibliographic aspect, there are varying degrees of interest in two main areas – modern first editions, as already stated, i.e. the relationship between jacket and book, but essential parts of the whole; and as an art form, particularly of the period when notable figures in the arts designed and illustrated jackets, from the middle 1920s to the 1950s. Early impact was made by distinguished names like Horace Brodzky whose stark style admirably captured the mood of serious novels such as Ben Hecht's *Gargoyles* and Theodore Dreiser's *Twelve Men* (c. 1919) yet was capable of humour that lifted the jacket of *The Curious Republic of Gondour* (c. 1919), by Samuel L. Clemens (Mark Twain).

In retrospect it seems remarkable that having taken so long to get the first exhibition of jackets in 1945 off the ground, practically another forty years were to elapse before the next significant exhibition was mounted, at Wolfson College, Oxford (1983); later to be repeated in a slightly different form at York. Entitled 'Saved from the wastepaper basket: British Book-Jackets 1925–1955', it was organised by David Alexander, a specialist in eighteenth century print, who happened to acquire a degree of expertise in this field through his book collecting activities. Alexander's main interest was in the artists and designers whose work was represented in what he regards as the 'golden age' of dust jackets.

In the catalogue he drew attention to the irony of today's more durable jackets (on coated paper) having a longer life while being in the main photographic or typographical, and so generally of less artistic interest than their predecessors. His impressions have not changed. 'Dust jackets have an impressively high nostalgic content,' he says today, 'important now that such a premium is put on period feeling, and it is often much easier to date a book from its jacket than from its typography.' I agree about the period 'feel' but have to point out that relatively few collectors are motivated by this consideration alone; no matter how attractive, the jacket remains an essential but complementary incentive, not the prime one.

Assessing the strides made in producing striking jackets after World War I, David Alexander maintains that it would not have been possible without 'the ready co-operation of some of the freshest talents of the day; artists of all kinds -- painters, printmakers, draughtsmen, illustrators, and commerical artists adept at designing posters on advertisements – were ready to take on the work.' In the catalogue, he wrote: 'In the immediate post-war period there was a strong feeling on the part of many artists that they should be more involved in commercial art as a means of bringing good design into the lives of millions of people.'

Alexander was able to describe the way jackets became an accepted way of developing a house style, e.g. Batsford for the use of strong colours by their in-house designer Brian Cook, using a method of colour printing called the Berté process which gave a more durable surface; Gollancz for the famous plain image, originally devised by typographer Stanley Morrison; and Faber's fiction identified with the powerful style of Barnett Freedman. (Alexander's biographical note reads: Freedman (1901–58), son of poor Russian immigrants to the East End of London, worked first for a monumental mason and then in an architect's office; later he went to St. Martins School of Art and the Royal College, where he subsequently taught. He hoped to earn his living as a painter but became best known for his commercial design and for his lithographs, especially for book jackets and illustrations.)

In the late thirties, a growing number of artists (they included men of the calibre of Edward Ardizzone – collected today for his book illustrations – and Lynton Lamb) began to base their illustrative designs on a careful study of the author's intentions, as opposed to symbolism, and Alexander indicates that this is true of the 1940s (although for a time wrappers almost disappeared because of the shortage of paper, and some publishers had to resort to using the unprinted sides of old jackets). The catalogue concluded with a brief reference to the post-war years.

New talents continued to be employed by the publishers, for example, that charming Gallic draughtsman Phillippe Jullian or Michael Ayrton, with his designs of disturbing strength. But, by and large, the best work had been done: the days when easel artists were prepared to undertake designs were nearly over. Instead there was more emphasis on the part of publishers upon very distinctive lettering. . . . Those publishers who continued to favour pictorial jackets increasingly used specialist illustrators, such as those who had regularly worked for *Radio Times*. But the majority have decided that the 'modern' thing to do is to rely on photographic and typographic covers, which, however well designed, cannot rival in interest the response of an artist to a commission.

The British bookseller who has had more experience of dust jackets and their history than most, is George Locke, best known as a specialist in SF and Fantasy, and early detective fiction. Like his American counterpart, Ken Leach, he has acquired his expertise the hard way, by being prepared to explore unknown territory, learning as he goes. Although book jackets are seldom sold on their own, no intelligent bookseller would ignore the opportunity to investigate anything that does come onto the market, which is how in 1978, Locke and a few rival dealers went to a Brighton bookshop offering the large collection of discarded wrappers from a long defunct rental library. The first thing he noticed was the absence of any obviously desirable material, such as jackets for early Agatha Christie and Edgar Wallace, but he did purchase nearly 300, mainly detective fiction, jackets for stock, and a half-dozen fantasy for his personal collection (see Chapter 4).

As I have shown it is often sensible to 'sit' on material that does not have an immediate sale, and that was Locke's initial reaction. However, as he recalled: 'There was the question of loyalty to my customers – some of whom would have the corresponding books in their collection and would dearly like to add the appropriate dust wrappers. They wouldn't thank me for being forced to buy the book a second time at, almost certainly, an altitudinous price. Then in hoping to match them with the corresponding books presented the problems of matching edition with edition, and condition with condition, apart from the sheer rarity of many of these books to be considered.'

Having decided to catalogue them there were no bibliographical details to which he could refer for guidance, so he had to do his own research. His experience is recorded in the journal *Antiquarian Book Monthly Review* (March 1979) under the headline: 'Dustwrappers & Sundry Confusions' from which the following extracts are taken:

My first step was to consider the printed price. The vast majority of novels published in the 20s and 30s were originally issued at 7/6. One or two coming out close to the end of the First World War were still issued at the 6s price which had been standard for the previous 20 years, while some appearing at the onset of the Second World War were emerging at 8/3 or more. A few books short on wordage emerged at lower prices such as 5s, while a few particularly bulky specimens came out at 8/6, 9/6 or 10/6. But the majority of library novels, including virtually all of the detective fiction were issued at 7/6.

What that means, where my divorced dustwrappers were concerned, was that specimens with the price of 7/6 *could* once have decorated first editions. Only *could*, for it was quite possible that a book might have gone through several editions at 7/6. . . . Many reprints carry reviews . . . which I either had to regard as a reprint, or at the very best (for a less popular book which may have had only one printing), to a later issue.

The absence of quoted reviews, however, was no guarantee of a first edition, but if other books by the same author were listed, and one or more of those was known to have been published after the title in question, then I could safely regard the dustwrapper as that of a reprint or a later issue. If the title was listed among those other books, I had to keep an open mind.

Lists of books by other authors also frequently appeared, and examination of those lists and collection of their publication with entries in the British Catalogue, the English Catalogue and other works was obviously necessary. In practice, I only troubled to go that far with the (very few) important dustwrappers. The lesser breed of writers, who made up the bulk of those novels, could reasonably be assumed to have enjoyed the proceeds of one printing only, and that if the dustwrapper showed no obvious signs that it belonged to a later edition or issue, I could reasonably safely declare it to be a first edition.

The next price level down was 3/6, and at first I automatically assumed them all to belong to cheaper editions or issues. . . . For a start, some titles were first issued at 3/6, such as R. Austin Freeman's *The Surprising Experiences of Mr Shuttlebury Cobb*, Gerard Fairlie's *Birds of Prey*, Francis Gerard's *Concrete Castle* and *The Black Emperor*, and Sydney Horler's *The Spy*. All those books declared the fact on their dustwrappers that they were first issued at that price. I was able to confirm from other sources that the Freeman and the Gerards *were* first issued at 3/6 and felt happy to take the other, less collectable, items at their face value.

I experienced one pitfall, however. Gerard's *The Black Emperor* had two impressions. The dustwrapper of one said 'new at 3/6' on the spine; the other 'entirely new at 3/6'. Which was the first? It so happened that the front flap of the former also said 'second impression', and so I was saved!

The investigation was further complicated by the variety of means in which the 3/6 price was incorporated – printed, overprinted, written on by hand, by label, that sometimes covered an original price. He asks how dustwrappers modified in these ways should be treated by the collector since they were, like as not, first edition dustwrappers at the start of their chequered careers? He answered as follows:

If the book had one printing but two issues, the second in a different binding, for example, then a collector should, if the order of issuance is known, place the 7/6 dustwrapper round the earlier and the 3/6 one around the later. But suppose the single printing had only one binding, and the collector had the opportunity to add the dustwrapper overprinted 3/6 to the book? Should he take it, or wait until the 7/6 one materialised? My personal answer to that problem – and it occurred two or three times with the dustwrappers I added to books in my collection – was to add (whichever), and make a careful note of what I'd done . . .

. . . The collection had two for William le Queux's *The White Glove*, identical save that one had the 7/6 price on the spine and front flap, the other none. Was it reasonable to suppose that if, say, 5,000 copies of the book were done, 5,000 unpriced dustwrappers would have been run off, a first batch being printed with 7/6 and a second batch destined for later printing and issuance at 3/6? And that the unpriced ones were advance copies for the reps to take round to potential buyers? My experience of very recent books, which are possible to check at source, suggests that this practice was very common.

If the scorn for book jackets shown by bibliographers for so many years is not due to mere snobbery, then George Locke's experience may throw some light on the matter – it is a chore which can often end in frustration. Furthermore, my own experience of checking bibliographical facts with publishers has, more often than not, been disappointing. There was a time when executives might spend a career with one firm which enabled them to remember such details, but the large turnover of staff today can mean that some members of staff know nothing about anything that does not appear in the current catalogue – even to the extent of denying that the book in question is one of theirs! On the other hand, one advantage of the cost-cutting measures of the 1980s, is that publishers make as few printing changes as possible, so that an original jacket is used for as long as possible, and since reprints may be as few as 500 to 750 copies, this is now even more likely!

Finally, there is the book jacket which, judging by the demand, might well have been made from the gold film; those that irrespective of any aesthetic qualities – attractive or downright ugly – are worth small fortunes matched with the first editions they adorn. No doubt if the early jackets of Fleming, Waugh, Lawrence or Greene were plain buff coloured and made from inferior paper of the quality of their nineteenth-century counterparts, they would still be in much demand. But, as it happens, some are not only good examples of the best in the genre, but have the added attraction of having been designed by – or had the blurbs written by the distinguished authors of the books they adorn.

It is known, for example, that D. H. Lawrence (1885–1930) wrote the blurb on the dust jacket of four of his titles, including the infamous *The Rainbow*, Methuen 1915, which was not only banned but had 1,011 copies destroyed by order of the magistrate. Having spent three years on this overlong (200,000 words) study of passionate relationship, Lawrence was understandably bitter by what he described as the 'capitulation' of his publishers without a fight, and would be equally horrified to learn how much one of these extremely rare first editions is worth today (even the early expurgated editions are scarce!); with the dust jacket it would probably go on to the market at many thousands of pounds.

Graham Greene is another who has written the blurb for at least a couple of his jackets – where he was not keen on what the publisher intended to use – for *A Burnt Out Case* and, probably, *Confidential Agent* (in a letter to the bookseller Rick Gekoski he says he thought he had made some for the latter, but could not be sure as he did not have a copy to hand to check). Nor is it generally realised that Evelyn Waugh designed the jackets for both *Vile Bodies* and *Decline & Fall*. Another valuable jacket is that for T. S. Eliot's *Old Possum's Book of Practical Cats,* Faber 1939 (the classic which inspired the musical production of 'Cats') because this was also designed by the author, and not as is generally believed Nicholas Bentley, who did the illustrations for the book. On a less elevated level the jacket for the best selling *A Postillion Struck By Lightning,* 1977, by Dirk Bogarde was also designed by the actor.

The average author does not have much influence on the design of jackets; in the past when production budgets were not so tight, it was different. It has even been suggested that Francis Cugat's striking painting for the jacket of Scott Fitzgerald's *The Great Gatsby* – showing a woman's face over an amusement park night scene – so fascinated the author that he saw her character in a new light, and made certain changes. But Fitzgerald's biographer Matthew Bruccoli is sceptical, indicating evidence that Fitzgerald did write the design of a *preliminary* jacket into the story, and may not have seen the 'new' one until after publication, when he described it as 'great'.

It is generally accepted now that jackets can add hundreds of pounds to the value of most collectable first editions – the amount varying according to the demand for that author. But when a writer is near the top of the collecting table, prices become astronomical. In an article in *Book & Magazine Collector* (September 1986), mention was made of the interest in Graham Greene first editions, saying that a copy of the first edition of *Brighton Rock* (1938) might fetch £100 without a jacket – and ten times that figure when complete. It went on to say '. . . even the least difficult early Greene, *Stamboul Train* (1932), which fetches £40–£50 without jacket, had recently been catalogued at £300 with . . .!' The writer was referring to Rick Gekoski who received five orders for this one copy. He might have been staggered to learn that Gekoski's autumn catalogue of that year, the same title – admittedly a presentation copy to Greene's mother-in-law, but without dust jacket – was offered at £1,500. Gekoski reckons that if he could find a first in fine jacket of *Brighton Rock* he would expect £3,000!

In the same catalogue, the price for Anthony Powell's *What's Become of Waring*, 1939, with a dust jacket that was slightly torn, was £1,875 simply because the jacket is so rare; and Waugh's *Vile Bodies* (the jacket featuring his own design) at £1,650. In this case the jacket was not fine, with a piece missing across the top of the spine and stained on the rear panel, but had the attraction of a presentation inscription to friends inside which includes the words 'For this body which you call vile, My Lord Jesus Christ was not ashamed to die.'

An added bonus is the additional 'wrap-around' paper band – usually a publisher's promotional device to announce some prize award – over the jacket. Fewer seem to survive and their presence adds 20%–30% to the value.

There is still an element of misguided snobbery among those who sneer at the obsession with fine dust jackets; people who point out in a very superior manner that books were meant to be *read* and not exhibited in an airtight glass case. At the same time there is some unnecessary confusion about what one does to protect a desirable jacket. I remember an auction of a valuable collection of lead soldiers, at least a couple of hundred years old. They had been in the possession of the vendor for twenty odd years, and in all that time they had been packed, individually wrapped in tissue paper, between cotton wool in boxes. Books, thank Heaven, have to be seen – but *how* surely depends on the collector. I do not know one bibliophile who keeps them locked away like toy soldiers; most of my acquaintances encase book and jacket in purpose-made cellophane jackets, rather like an updated public library casing; some remove the more valuable jackets for safe keeping; replacing them with home-made brown paper covers; and some leave their greatest treasures on the shelves, alongside reprints and even paperbacks. To be reading this book at all, means that you will already be familiar with the common-sense dos-and-don'ts of protecting any paper-based material against the dangers of sunlight, humidity, atmospheric pollution and extremes of temperature.

However, once a jacket has been damaged in some way, it needs the attention of an experienced conservator. It is tempting to repair small nicks with cellotape on the underside, but this should be resisted, because the area eventually turns brown, quite apart from any deterioration of the paper caused by chemical agents in the adhesive. In fact, with professional help there is little that cannot be done to restore a dust jacket to its former glory – such as 'invisible' repairs, getting rid of most stains and marks, and colours matched and re-created – but there is a growing resistance now among conservators to what they regard as 'cosmetic' treatment, as opposed to essential preservation (see Chapter 7); fortunately there are still a number who will be happy to do the work, although it makes sense to check their credentials first!

Seven

PRESERVING THE PAST – AND FUTURE

Every bibliophile appreciates the growing importance of book preservation. But pressed for a definition of the term 'preservation', the response may be somewhat bemused.

'Preservation? . . . preventing very old books from disintegrating . . .'

'Conservation?'

'That's right.'

'Restoration?'

'Yes, same thing . . .'

But it isn't. In fact, all three words have different meanings, and although the editors of a thesaurus might be excused for lumping them together – and to the layman the differences are insignificant – serious collectors should have a much clearer picture of the work that is being carried out today in the race against time to save much of our cultural heritage.

Gone are the days, before the panic button was pressed, when it was a newsworthy event for a library or museum to entrust a particularly gifted craftsman with the repair of a masterpiece – an early manuscript or binding in danger of falling to pieces. Because of their in-depth knowledge of the history of book structure and of the characteristics of early vellum, it was invariably the gifted hand binders who took on these tremendous responsibilities – craftsmen like Douglas Cockerell, invited by the British Museum in 1935 to rebind its recently acquired *Codex Sinaiticus*, the fourth-century Greek manuscript of the bible.

That all changed when it was noticed that many very old books – handbound and with paper made in the traditional way from rags – were standing up to the ravages of time better than those dating

141

from the mid-nineteenth century when, because of the desperate need for paper to meet the book explosion, manufacturers 'discovered' wood pulp. What they did not realise was that the process introduced a self-destructive high acid content – causing damage that has been compounded over the years. We are talking not only of old books, but those just off the presses. Acidic elements in the wood pulp begin to eat away at the finished paper even before it gets to the publisher; other chemicals contained in size, for example, attack over a longer period the fibres which give paper its body.

Research has developed at a snowballing pace since the British Library linked up with The British Leather Manufacturers' Research Association in 1976 in a joint programme to investigate the causes of leather decay, and methods of treating new skins and leathers covering existing bindings. The results, published in 1984 by The British Library are too technical for inclusion in my necessarily superficial study, but coupled with similar research on both sides of the Atlantic, make an invaluable contribution to the piece-by-piece solution of a vast and escalating problem.

Tackling the even more urgent headaches of paper deterioration, The British Library Research and Development department in 1982/83 financed a project supervised by Dr Fred Ratcliffe at Cambridge University. The report 'formally' confirmed what had disturbed conservation experts for years – the basic lack of knowledge and, equally important, the absence of any co-ordination of research carried out by libraries and universities working independently. Ratcliffe's findings led to the setting up in 1984 of a National Preservation Office, housed at the British Library. The NPO immediately embarked on an education programme which, obvious though it may seem, is a massive undertaking when dealing with modern book production and the vast output of new books.

Another project is the compilation of a national register to minimise duplication in microfilming rare works, while another investigates the possibility of strengthening paper by 'bonding' it with polymer fibres. In 1986 the office launched a 'survival kit' dispensing information on all relevant topics, with practical hints to collectors and librarians on where and how books should be stored, how to dust and clean, etc. They even introduced full and part-time courses in conservation.

Conscious as society is today of such environmental hazards as acid rain, it seems incredible that warnings about potential dangers inherent in the atmosphere – even dust, which may even contain mould spores – were being received more than a century ago, e.g. Derôme (Léopold), *Le Luxe des Livres*, Paris 1879. Apart from light (natural and artificial), temperature and humidity, elements that can be harmful to book materials include a variety of pollutants synonymous with industrialised society, such as sulphur dioxide – not in itself harmful but which in moist conditions and in the presence of iron forms sulphuric acid, which is very harmful.

Nor is the concept of conservation new. As early as 1901, Douglas Cockerell wrote in *Bookbinding and the Care of Books* (with reprints, probably the most widely read book on the subject): 'Sheets of very old books are best left with the stains upon them except perhaps, such as can be removed with hot water or size. Nearly all stains can be removed, but in the process old paper is apt to lose more in character than it gains in appearance.'

Because of the wide range of problems surrounding the preservation of deteriorating books and manuscripts (and photo and film stock) the degrees of emphasis on the importance of one approach as against another will continue to fluctuate over the years. In the problems of structure it may well remain the province of the craftsman; of chemical contamination that of the scientist, but first comes the need to understand the different work classifications because of the amount of overlapping and (surprising to the outsider) the very strong differences of opinion among experts as to what is the 'correct' approach.

In broad terms, *Preservation* means what it sounds like: to use preventative measures and methods of protection to prevent an artefact from deteriorating further, i.e. work done is in the 'passive' sense, because there is no physical activity.

Conservation means stabilisation work, such as washing and de-acidification, and which might involve the inclusion of a small amount of new materials (i.e. for support/strengthening) rather than replacement of earlier material.

Restoration means to restore to a semblance of the original with the addition where essential of new materials replacing the original, although this is more likely in the case of repair.

Unfortunately, there are grey areas and the controversy arises over what might be called the 'integrity' of the original. An extreme example might be to 'pull' (i.e. to unpick) a disintegrating book with broken spine of (say) the seventeenth century with its distinctive binding style, and simply re-sew and re-back the content in the fashion of a modern book. No one could justify that thoughtless sort of repair, but the extreme wing of the conservators' lobby believe that *any* deviation from the original is wrong. If change is essential to prevent a book from falling to pieces, they say, there must be no attempt to conceal it.

This philosophy sounds reasonable, in theory – if working for a library or museum, but most collectors or dealers do not want to apologise for a spate of repairs. Indeed, most libraries find compromise acceptable, and I know of one which asked a conservator to repair an old volume bound in alum tawed pigskin (not only very durable but because of the chemical process resistant to polluted atmospheres). This leather is snowy white at the outset but age changes it to a shade of cream or ivory and because the craftsman's philosophy was that his work had to be clearly seen as a repair he rebacked it in a new piece of leather – in dazzling white. The contrast with front and back covers was so startling that the customer approached another expert to have the spine toned down.

And talking of spines – at the other end of the spectrum – one of the leading authorities on the subject, an historian as well as craftsman-binder, Bernard Middleton believes it is fair to restore a book as near as possible to the original . . . to the extent that if he is putting on a new strip of leather he will add scrapings of old leather to match up. While he would not interfere with a book's structure* he cannot see anything wrong in restoration. 'What I do is more difficult and considerably more bother,' he points out, 'and if you look carefully you can always see the repair. Although I aim to make changes imperceptible, I know that it is a standard I will very rarely achieve. It is my way of trying to maintain an acceptable level of craftsmanship.'

While such philosophical debate among experts is fascinating, we must not lose sight of the magnitude of the task facing the men

---

*There might be exceptions, e.g. many nineteenth century books were given hollow backs even though they were not functionally necessary. In such cases he might make it into a tight back to strengthen the structure.

and women charged with the preservation of priceless or irreplaceable material. Roger Powell, one of the world's most respected craftsmen, at ninety still admits to having his heart in his mouth every time he tackles a new assignment, and it would be a fool who did not face each new challenge with some apprehension. A mistake made in a routine repair might be annoying, but when that work is being carried out on something unique, the damage could be irrevocable. Imagine the horror of the person cleaning with a damp sponge, a vellum scroll containing the seal and signature of King John, when the inked signature lifted off and began to disintegrate! That catastrophe actually happened; the surprise is that similar misfortunes do not occur more frequently, given the volatile nature of ink and the fragility of deteriorating paper.

Indeed, there is a strong body of opinion among conservators that it is better to wait for chemical research to come up with more answers before experimenting with important material. Caution is advocated by Don Etherington, for example, Chief Conservation Officer at the HRC laboratories.

There has been a tremendous amount of research in the past decade which has shed new light on the techniques and practices of conservation, notably on such areas as cellulose and leather deterioration, de-acidication and alkalisation processes, light bleaching, chemical bleaching, media analysis and washing with water. Problems with conservation techniques are often known to exist even before the reasons for the problems. In view of the tremendous amount of damage ('mistakes' on a large scale) which has occurred in the past as a result of the application of systems which are imperfectly understood (lamination and bleaching are prime examples) the suggestion that a little more time be spent on attempting to understand the scientific principles behind the techniques being used should not be interpreted as being based on unreasonable fear.

Most natural deterioration process are not extremely rapid. There is a lot of good which can be accomplished towards the preservation of an item simply by moving it from poor housing to good housing. Conservators should not attempt to perform treatments the results of which can not be anticipated if there are alternative solutions which will both achieve sound preservation goals and allow additional time to more thoroughly investigate the nature of the problems they are facing. Additionally, and specifically in large collections, there are a tremendous number of items which will benefit from currently understood treatments. No conservator will need to sit idle because there is nothing which can currently be done to conserve the collection.

Sometimes action *has* to be taken, either because the problems are urgent, and because of the need for access to the artefact, e.g. in 1986 Don Etherington's own expert staff had to prepare two irreplaceable properties in time for exhibition as part of Texas's 150th independence celebrations, i.e. the declaration itself announcing the State's independence from Mexico, and the six page 'I shall never surrender or retreat' letter written a week earlier (February 1836) by Colonel William B. Travis, commander of the heroic defenders of the Alamo.

Careful examination of the brittle documents revealed that the declaration had at some time in the past undergone 'silking', an outdated preservation process whereby starch paste was spread over a paper's surface and fine silk pressed on to it – the problem being that both silk and paste deteriorate, creating additional problems for future preservation. Action which had to be taken included reinforcing weakened edges, mending 'fractures' in the paper, and using a chemical solution to leave an alkaline buffer to offset acidity attacks; finally the documents were fitted into frames containing a special plexiglas to retard ultraviolet light.

There is, of course, no substitute for experience; the more problems encountered by a craftsman the fewer surprises he can expect. Apprenticeships, during which every aspect of a craft is studied in depth, have become a relic of the past. Companies and institutions can no longer afford to pay a living wage to youngsters 'merely' for training – that is, for so little immediate return, and coupled with the high costs of materials it means that there is no scope for the teaching of specialist techniques such as hand colouring, something which used to be routine.

Alf Brazier, for example, conservation consultant to the British Museum (apart from the British Library, each department of the museum has its own specialist book collection), was trained in the days when a seven-year apprenticeship was standard. And since after making the grade his experience includes twenty years teaching at the London College of Printing, and seven years in conservation with the Middlesex County Records Office, he had had his share of heart-stopping moments. One was reminiscent of the disappearance of the King John signature. A student trying to remove an iron stain from a large nineteenth-century poster, a fairly routine operation, immersed the poster in a tray of bleach. He forgot the poster and by the time he looked again, the printer's ink was beginning to rise off the paper!

The bleach had to be removed, but Brazier knew that if the plug was removed or the tray tipped even slightly, the floating ink would disappear. Without disturbing the tray he carefully drilled holes in the bottom – partially plugging them with matchsticks so that the bleach trickled out very slowly. When the ink had sunk back on the paper, it was sealed with a vellum size. Once secure, the poster was washed to get rid of the bleach, re-sized and finally pressed.

Obviously, the more experienced the craftsman, the less likely is he or she to make significant mistakes; and since human error can never be ruled out the better able to cope with such disasters. Brazier recalls an occasion when the laboratory staff under his supervision was asked to restore an old and valuable atlas from the contents of two damaged copies. The flawed volumes were very carefully dismantled; the better pages repaired and cleaned, and the 'new' atlas sewn for rebinding. Although not especially complicated, the result of many hours of intricate and skilled work was highly satisfactory, and thoughts were turning to the next job when the machine operator had an 'accident' with the guillotine – slipping up some steps and dropping the book which slid on to the work-bench and over to the 'start' button. The book was sliced in two! Fortunately, the client had not asked for the return of the rejected sheets, so the whole process was laboriously repeated – with satisfactory results.

'Problems like these might arise only once in a lifetime,' Mr Brazier points out, 'but it does mean that you would know what to do if did happen again. Some people come into conservation after a one- or two-year course, and imagine they know it all.'

Having somewhat confusingly bracketed conservation and restoration to make a point about the skill entailed in both areas, it might be appropriate at this stage to investigate some of the differences.

Some conservators adopt such a high moral tone that they believe the term 'restoration' should apply to fine art; that any attempt to 'improve' or return a book to its original state, reduces its status to no more than a facsimile. Such apparent outrage is a legacy of early examples in which, mainly through ignorance, invaluable information on the original construction of books, was destroyed, in the main by bookbinders. In the seventeenth and eighteen centuries, not only was original craftsmanship ripped apart without a second thought, but some of the binding and paper used as scrap for building up the new leather covers. I remember seeing a small, rather nondescript book – *The Art of English Poetry* by Edward Bysshe, published in 1714 – which in appearance did not merit more than a fleeting glance. But when the binding came to be repaired 'waste' material found sandwich-fashion between leather and board, and between board and paste-down, turned out to be sheets from *Bartholaeus Anglicus*, quarto, printed in Westminster in 1495 by Wynkyn de Worde, Caxton's worthy successor.

'Worthy' is an understatement, yet history has not always been kind to Wynkyn de Worde, as was recalled in the following grim anecdote from William Blades, in *The Enemies of Books*, London 1880, which as the title implies is required reading for any conservator, dealing with every hazard from fire to worms. Blades describes how a friend took lodgings at a house in Brighton, where in the toilet he found some leaves of a very old book. '. . . He asked permission to retain them, and enquired if there were any more where they came from. Two or three other fragments were found, and the landlady stated that her father, who was fond of antiquities, had at one time a chest full of old black letter (Gothic type) books; that, upon his death, they were preserved until she was tired of seeing them, and then, supposing them of no value, she had used them for waste; that for two years and a half they had served for various household purposes, including toilet paper, but she had just come to the end of them.

The fragments preserved, and now in my possession, are a goodly portion of one of the most rare books from the press of

Wynkyn de Worde. The title is a curious woodcut with the words 'Gesta Romanorum' engraved in an odd-shaped black letter. It has also numerous rude woodcuts throughout. It was from this very work that Shakespeare in all probability derived the story of the three caskets in which 'The Merchant of Venice' forms so integral a portion of the plot. Only think of that sewer being supplied daily with such dainty bibliographical treasures!

A diet of such horror stories is enough to make any book lover a willing recruit for a potential Bibliophiles Liberation Army, but fortunately not all conservators are necessarily aggressive; those with the highest reputation for integrity as well as skill and knowledge, tend to be more moderate in their views. One such person is Christopher Clarkson of the Bodleian Library, who although believing that the book is an inviolable physical object, recognises that there are a number of grey areas – such as whether or not there is any intention to deceive; whether or not there is appreciation of the value of the period object. Restoration is not necessarily a bad thing, he concedes, unless it moves too close to facsimile making.

Clarkson's philosophy is outlined in a paper 'The Conservation of Early Books in Codex Form' for the Institute of Paper Conservation published in 1978 but still appropriate. In it, he argues the need for achieving a balanced conservation programme for which aesthetic and historical awareness can no longer be neglected:

> . . . The roots of such problems may stem from the basic attitudes and trade character of the bookbinding craft, attitudes formed and encouraged by buyers and dealers in antiquarian books who, except in rare cases, have not been noted for their historical sensitivity as much as for their business acumen. Consequently books have often suffered from restoration (rather than conservation) and rebinding practices which were bad for the former, but good for the latter. To the dealer, the basic characteristics of a saleable item has been in the past as it is today – 'good' to 'excellent' condition. This attitude has led to the practice of 'tidying up' an item, encouraging such practices as 'pulling', washing/cleaning, bleaching, rebinding, etc, to the cheapest price. A few enlightened collectors and rare book

librarians in recent years have attempted to buy particular items before restoration. However, tidy mindedness and over restoration are still the main destroyers of period books.

It is useful to return my essentially broad definition of the terms of reference earlier in the chapter, to illustrate the differences of *emphasis* in the approach of experts on both sides of the argument. Mr Clarkson believes that 'restoration' simply means 'substantial interference and/or replacement of period materials in an artefact.' His philosophy in a nutshell is as follows: 'The idea which underlies my use of the word "preservation" and "conservation" is to delay restoration for as long as possible. "Preservation" is preventive measures and conservation is the process of making safe and usable an object which has become fragile, using minimum interference.'

In the IPC paper, he deals at length with education.

Although codicology or the 'archaeology' of the book is still a young science and at present concerned with the manuscripts of the Medieval period, its short life has markedly altered the way books in general are seen and studied. The new discipline is beginning to unify bibliographical specialities and in doing so is producing an overriding awareness of the need for the preservation of the integral object.

During the last few years of my work as a conservator, I have begun to record and file all my notes concerning materials and techniques of binding construction under the wide umbrella, 'codicology'. In doing so I am aware I am stretching the subject beyond the bounds of Medieval manuscript production, but I feel that the separation which has occurred between late manuscripts and early printed book studies must not find an echo in my conservation work notes and studies. Indeed the task of bringing together all these now separate disciplines concerned with the book as a physical object, into an understandable harmony, belongs to the present generation.

In the gathering of knowledge, it becomes increasingly difficult for binders or conservators to anticipate what will be the most important aspects of any particular volume to future scholarship, and therefore it becomes difficult to say correspondingly what information must be available to conservators in order to make a professional judgement. As with any other art object, early books with their diverse materials and techniques warrant careful, individual study and attention. Book conservation is a discipline which has gone largely unnoticed by the conservation world in general, possibly because the majority of early books are housed in libraries and archives rather than museums and galleries. The general approach towards such objects is entirely different in museums than in libraries and is a reflection of different philosophical approaches to preservation and conservation. So relatively new is interest in the production of books of all periods, compared with other areas of bibliographical research, that important losses still are occurring frequently within our major libraries.

Defining the codex book as 'an object constituted of multiple and separate components, gatherings, text-blocks, binding construction, covering, metal furniture, fastenings, etc,' Clarkson explains: 'Combined, these form numerous subtleties of historical interest and theoretical evidences, indicating period fashion and provenance; divided, they lose much of their meaning and power to conjure human thought. Bibliographical integrity is not something one can dismantle and recreate. The whole entity of the object from its conception through every phase of its long history, creates a spell which can be shattered so easily by any encroachment. What needs to be preserved of the physical aspect of an historic object is the inexplicable, the spontaneous and the unconscious qualities inherent in the particular age; but by their very nature these are the most difficult qualities to retain in any conservation procedure and almost completely impossible if one is forced to rebind a volume. In other words, command over technical complexity, while requiring patience and skill, has little or no relationship to the creative or spontaneous artistry of one's own age, let alone of another age.'

Relating a book to an inviolable physical object, in the context of historical integrity, is not dissimilar to the artistic statement made by the trend-setting modern bookbinder, Ivor Robinson, who is almost alone among his contemporaries in believing that (in a 'new' work as opposed to restoration of an old book) a modern binding should stand on its own. The more commonly held belief is that the binder's role is to interpret, express or even develop the author's 'message'. Robinson maintains that the author is frequently just one contributor to the total book – no more important than the person who made the paper, selected and set the print, or did the illustrations.

Drawing a parallel with the protection of old buildings Clarkson concedes:

> While any encroachment by the restorer tends to lessen the learning value to the bibliographer of the original, certain activities have to be carried out to assure an object's stability and continued preservation. Rebinding may prove to be the only alternative in some cases, but guidelines must be firmly established.

The preservation of library collections has grown into a huge and complex business in itself, already separating into specialised branches, not overwhelmingly concerned with the preservation of information still mainly carried upon paper support material and bound in codex form. Preservation of library materials has become a subject where, of necessity (and because of its youth), large generalisations are made and solutions to particular problems quickly become semi-mass production methods which, as the phrase suggests, often do not take into account the techniques and materials of individual items. Unfortunately, with the poor state of our present knowledge of materials and structures, and limited means of circulating what knowledge we have, such attitudes and methods are spilling over into the far smaller area of rare books and special collections, where I am not convinced they belong, and on into the even smaller world of early manuscripts and printed books, where such attitudes definitely do not belong.

On the ethics of book conservation, Clarkson says:

> The respect required for books is particularly demanding, for books present complex problems unique unto themselves; books unlike most paintings and prints, are three dimensional, mechanical portable objects. A term such as 'book conservation' to me cannot imply simply the repair of text-block and rebinding for use in a 20th century library. It implies also the restoration of qualities of movement such as ease of opening, spine flexibility

and leaf flow. The conservation problems of a book are possibly unique because they entail reactivating the materials which form the moving parts of the object. To restore qualities of movement is easier said than done, for one must rejuvenate the large number and wide variety of materials which go into the make-up of books. One's concerns are not only with paper and covering leathers but also with other skin products and with wood, textiles and metals, all of which are in close juxtaposition, some even entwined with one another, each affecting its neighbour chemically and physically, making strict environment balance, care in handling and conservation treatments essential. Often the desire to restore a book to its original function has resulted in destroying its character, the resultant object changing into a useless hybrid.

The answer to the problem of restoration of such physical qualities as movement and flexibility too often has been rebinding. So slight is the appreciation of bindings in some library areas that even scholarly writings and assessments cannot always ensure the survival of important binding structures. If we wish to preserve rather than destroy historic books, then rebuilding and rebinding must gradually become a far smaller part of the total preservation programme. Instead, refurbishing and rejuvenation must be promoted to a major priority, with their own research and development programme. It is a fact that one often gives thanks to past librarians' very crude methods of patching and wrapping bindings, for at least the original material is underneath rather than replaced.

The present rather free use of the word 'conservation' when applied to rebinding practices disturbs me. In the museum conservation of objects, materials are treated so they are safe to be displayed, stored and handled by a few trained hands. Restoration of the object to its original function is never intended. When applied to bookbindings the word should have a similar meaning. In fact, the word conservation should not be associated with rebinding practices at all, for it denotes first and foremost a middle ground lying between preservation measures and complete replacement. The control over the future use of an artefact is of major importance when determining whether a work can be limited to conservation treatments alone.

Unfortunately, philosophically we suffer still from the restoration mentality. This is soon shown by the low priority given to research in the area of preventative preservation and general maintenance, as opposed to the too ready acceptance of replacement and rebinding. Once a volume has deteriorated to the point of obviously requiring restoration, then it must be clearly understood that however carefully such work is executed the volume will lose a certain amount of its integral worth, an irreparable loss to future scholarship. Conservators must accept the responsibility in our projected treatment proposals to state clearly and fairly what will be the likely effect of the proposed work on the period integrity of the volume – a task for which there is never enough knowledge.

He makes the point that nothing should be taken for granted; that every scrap of evidence is important.

I find that it is impossible to collect even the most rudimentary information concerning the significance of a particular volume, e.g. How many like volumes remain intact? What condition are they in? Are they in public or private ownership? Even information bearing more directly upon the uniqueness of a volume to future bibliographical studies is difficult to come by. It is one of its type, or one of fifty, in a given area? Indicators of provenance, evidence of its adventures along with other features which constitute the uniqueness of the volume, are all vital pieces of information and should be available during the decision-making process.

From the technical point of view, knowledge of historical binding practices, spanning the whole chronology of the codex with all its cultural variations, should also grow in importance. One only need study a particular region and period of bookbinding to realise how important such information is to the developing field of early book preservation . . . Only now with the rise of archaeological attitudes within book studies do I find hope of a unifying influence, because this approach at least focuses upon material technology and book construction. We still do not have the knowledge to form such a data bank, or even to form an endangered species list, which is such a major priority.

Mr Clarkson is also concerned with the 'reversibility' principle – the concept, accepted in art conservation circles, but not so much in the book world, that such work has a certain life expectancy.

Certainly we cannot have confidence that the materials available to us are as good as, or an improvement upon, the materials being replaced. For example, compare the appearance of leather used for rebacking in the 19th and 20th centuries with the ageing qualities of earlier leathers? In the past twenty-five years the general standards of hand-made paper, book cloth and leathers available to us have dropped measurably. In many instances I find that I can no longer justify the use of materials which may only last, let us say, fifty years, while a life expectancy of 150–250 years may be thought by the custodians as the only justification for the many hours spent on repairs. Even with badly damaged early books, provided their storage environment is good and their handling is both educated and limited, it can be argued that a holding operation is best, at least until such time as the development of new materials and the beginning renaissance in 'hand crafted' materials have improved to the point of making their use viable. This means that there is an ethical obligation to contribute in every way possible to the improvement of the materials we use.

. . . Until recent years librarians and custodians of rare and important books have encouraged free use with little or no handling education attempted. The devastation caused by such policies and still being caused in many institutions is a disgrace. In such circumstances, the conservator is forced to replace much historical material and evidence so that the volume will stand up to excessive and rigorous use.

Summing up, he concludes:

There is in vogue a view that the craftsmanship necessary for the conservation and restoration of bindings can be neutral, unbiased or divorced from our present age. I fear this can lead to an unsympathetic and sterile treatment of historic objects, as has happened when the pendulum has swung too far towards purely

155

'chemists' restoration; also that this movement has also contributed to the idea that a facsimile could be used as substitute for the original. Of course, it cannot because the original has 'life', a depth sufficient to conjure the emotions, and be open to changing interpretations. The argument that the public cannot tell the difference is insidious; one that rudely limits the human spirit and search for knowledge to the narrow confines of our own personal understanding or lack of it.

Many of the complaints of ignorance among some binders are echoed by Bernard Middleton, who has published a study of English historical trade techniques, is the author of *The Restoration of Leather Bindings*, American Library Association, (Chicago 1972, rev. 1984), and whose definition of restoration I have already summarised. In the preface to the first edition of the above book, he declares that repairs should be as unobtrusive as is compatible with reasonable strength (and obviously, stopping short of falsification). Elaborating, he says:

Complete and unthinking adherence (to the no interference principle) in every detail is not vital. It seems to me that if a sliver of new leather is let into one end of a slightly cracked joint and this is done more for the sake of appearance than for structural gain, no harm has been done if the repair is undetectable. On the other hand, one should hesitate to add a tooled and artifically aged lettering piece to a binding if the binding had not been lettered in the first place; apart from any other considerations, such an addition might confuse.

Between these two extremes there is much that calls for the application of common sense and discretion. Temptations are numerous because a great many owners of books want them 'doctored' undetectably for one reason or another. The craftsman's pride is another hazard because he may well be regarded as incompetent if he does not comply with the owner's instructions. Maximum strength and period fidelity are two sometimes conflicting factors which the conscientious restorer must constantly endeavour to balance.

No one would question the integrity of a restorer of Middleton's status, but it is worth drawing attention to the great detail in which he advises other craftsmen when approaching areas of controversy. When inserting new endpapers, for example, even where genuinely old (most restorers keep stocks of dated paper salvaged from destroyed and useless books), he describes the way in which they can be stained and then appropriately 'aged' by the application of dust rubbed into treated cotton wool; how an unnaturally 'hard' or sharp look of newly-cut pages can be softened by lightly scraping while damp with a knife. (NB: These tips are taken out of context merely to illustrate a point – so please don't try to copy!)

He believes that the use of such techniques is not a matter of faking or attempting to deceive anyone, but of creating harmony between the pastedown, the flyleaf and the book by softening the unnatural starkness of the new leaves. 'It should be stated,' he points out, 'that some conservators are opposed to this procedure on the grounds that the dirt may be acidic and therefore harmful to the paper.

'If the restorer is concerned that the inserted end papers are likely to give rise to confusion as to their originality, especially if old paper is used, I suggest that the simulated staining from the turn-ins be made to deviate somewhat from the edges of the leather. This provides the bibliographer with proof that the endpapers are not original and will not give offence because the average owner will not notice the slight discrepancy.'

Another common complaint about some restorers is that they 'automatically' re-sew books, in the interests of appearance and strength. In his book, Bernard Middleton advises the student that every alternative be explored first, e.g. to sew new cords *over* the old, forming new slips for reattaching the boards. Apart from the question of preserving the integrity of a period artefact, re-sewing can result in uneven page edges, and cause the book to lose its original 'feel'. Where paper guards for each section are incorporated (to prevent glue from coming into contact with the folds of the text-block and eventually damaging them when the book is again re-sewn in years to come, and to facilitate ease of opening) the repaired back can be thicker than the leather spine due to be put back. Noting the need for compromise he will use a home-made paste before glueing, because as already stated it was often the glue which had done the damage (pre-mid sixteenth-century bindings, before glue was introduced, are easier to 'pull' for re-sewing than those of later centuries).

Bernard Middleton applauds the lead taken by Christopher Clarkson in demanding new standards of knowledge. Maintaining detailed notes of work carried out is one rule they have in common, the following supplied by him being a typical example (typed on good, strong *acid-free paper*) and tipped in at the back of the book:

THE THEATRE OF THE EMPIRE OF GREAT BRITAINE
By John Speed, London, 1676
Bound in contemporary panelled calf

When received, the outer joints of this book were broken, the boards were detached, the corners of the boards were badly damaged, and the final eleven plates were detached from their guards. The book had been re-endpapered with marbled paper over the original plain ones, apparently early in the nineteenth century. The sewing structure was sound but the headbands were missing.

Treatment

The loose plates were replaced on their guards. The book was reheadbanded, rebacked, and the corners were stiffened with paste, built up with wood paste, and repaired with new leather. The marbled paper covering the old pastedowns was removed. The flyleaves were replaced with matching seventeenth-century paper. Attachment of the boards was reinforced with overcast cloth joints which have been concealed under the original pastedowns. The original spine was replaced over the new.

PVA was used to stick down the cloth joints; otherwise, boiled wheat flour paste containing thymol was employed throughout. The binding has been treated with a 7 per cent solution of potassium lactate in distilled water with 0.25 per cent paranitrophenol added to protect against mould, and with a leather dressing consisting of 60 per cent neat's foot oil and 40 per cent anhydrous lanolin.

signed and dated

Middleton suggests that if a tooled spine or side cannot be saved, it is a good plan to take a rubbing of it with a soft pencil on thin paper, and attach it with the note. Any interesting features which are going to be lost or covered by the restoration should also be noted and, ideally, photographed. For a particularly important book much more extensive documentation may be desirable.

Typical of the scholarly information needed for older books, such as *The Carisbrook Cartularly* of 1150AD conserved and repaired for the British Library by Roger Powell in 1950, which I saw at an exhibition to commemorate the ninetieth birthday of Powell, by the Crafts Council in 1986. Accompanying the work were his notes:

> Binding much broken down and only a fragment of the leather covering to the spine remained. Back edges of boards badly damaged by 'furniture beetle'. Leaves very badly cockled and a number of them torn. The sewing was normal 'herring bone', catching up the stitches of the previous section at each of the white leather thongs which (double) thongs were laced into Poplar boards.
>
> There were indications that the book had been sewn previously. Sections (a) and (n) were clearly added after the book had been in use for some time without boards, and front leaf (b) and last leaf (m). The headbands were sewn over white leather thongs (using a linen thread independent of the main sewing) and laced in to the boards.
>
> All the leaves have been flattened as follows: Two new vellum leaves with white alum tawed goatskin joints have been added at each end, sewn on three double cords at the old holes and on two additional cords through a continuous zigzagging of handmade paper.
>
> All the cords have been laced into the original boards which have had their inner edges replaced by Agba (joint made with 'Beetle', synthetic glue) and have been treated with woodworm destroyer. The spine has been covered with 'Hermitage' calf protected with a seven per cent solution of potassium lactate. Old sides replaced. Label from old spine pasted on new.

It was Roger Powell who in 1953 repaired and rebound the eighth century *Book of Kells* for Trinity College Library, Dublin. This illuminated vellum manuscript of the Gospels had been bound as one volume in the previous century, and Powell's commission was to prepare four separately bound volumes without

159

any alteration to the original manuscript. He noted: 'Because the Board of Trinity College would not allow any thinning from the spine edges, the necessary mending of the spine folds produced enormous and intolerable swelling* at the spine. To overcome this, four leaves of blank vellum as single guards were inserted between each section. Because of the ban on the thinning of spine edges, repair of the spine folds was accomplished by using fine unbleached linen.'

Beset by many of the problems of the paper conservators are the men and women who specialise in the preservation of photographic materials; indeed, even more complex because of the presence of emulsions and other organic materials. The question of ethics – what treatment can, or should not be carried out – is just as fiercely debated, although simplified to some extent by the physical limitations on what can be added to a negative or print, as opposed to a 'restored' book – although it was not uncommon for original glass plates to be destroyed once copy negatives have been made!

The subject should be of special interest to us; we tend to forget that one of the driving forces behind photographic pioneering was the desire to see photographs produced *en masse* through the medium of the book. Although photography is a modern science – or perhaps *because* of its rapid emergence – an awareness of the need to extend and preserve the life of photographic images came before it dawned on the bookworld (e.g. Derôme's warning in 1879). The main causes of deterioration were outlined in the Committee of Image Permanence, headed by Thomas Hardwick as early as 1851. However, technical discoveries and innovation are one thing; what has been done in the name of technical 'ingenuity' is another. In the view of Ian and Angela Moor, consultants to the British Library's Department of Printed Books, and leading authorities in the United Kingdom:

> Every conservation and restoration discipline has very rigid standards, ethics and principles. This necessary self-imposed morality is designed to protect the artefact from misuse and malpractice detrimental to its continued longevity, and to preserve all intrinsic and integral characteristics. A clear distinction must be made between what is acceptable for the

*The vellum leaves were 'washed', flattened and repaired before rebinding.

photographer to do in the initial production of his work and what is acceptable for the conservator whose job it is to preserve all the essential characteristics and integrity of the photographer's work; not to change them nor, in his vanity, try to improve upon them.

The Moors' speciality is nineteenth-century (i.e. 1839–1900) photography, but they have considerable experience in working with paper. At one time they also did a fair amount of repairs to graphic media, e.g. dust jackets – until coming to the conclusion that much of the work, especially 'touching up' colours, was cosmetic, and as such divorced from the real problems of conservation (a philosophy which has much in common with that of Christopher Clarkson of the Bodleian).

In an article 'The Imperfect Image' published in *The Photograhic Collector*, Vol. 3, No. 2, in 1982, the Moors outline the complexity of the problems to be faced. 'Photographs exist on four distinct levels and they are prone to degradation on each, which makes them unique. The external factors affecting this degradation are: environmental, physical and contaminants. Internal factors are: residual chemicals, migratory contaminants and physical incompatabilities. Therefore, we must not consider the influences of degradation as a totality; we must consider the inherent qualities of the materials being affected too.

1. The base or support material. This can be either paper, glass, metal, leather, wood, fabric, bone or ceramic, and these materials will react independently to the image-bearing colloids (e.g. emulsion), inducing physical incompatabilities.
2. The image bearing colloids if present can be albumen, collodion or gelatine and all of these materials are degradable as a direct result of their inherent qualities, e.g. albumen has a natural free sulphur element in its composition; collodion-nitrated cellulose is susceptible to both chemical and physical degradation; gelatine is susceptible to high humidity, mould attack and acid and alkaline conditions. Again these materials will react independently to their support.
3. The photographic image for all intents and purposes is classified as a work of art, but unlike its counterpart the painting or drawing, it cannot effectively be restored using the same

161

mediums that produced it.

4. Finally, it is ironic that it is the deliberate degradation of known sensitive materials by light and chemical agents that give rise to the phenomenon known as a photograph, and yet, it is these very same agents which must be controlled in order to prevent photographs from being degraded to the point of destruction.'

The sensitivity of the medium in which they work is such that the risks of losing certain original qualities through treatment that might be regarded as philistine or unethical, is even greater than in book conservation. One of the most common hazards is caused through image intensification. In 1983, a number of nineteenth-century images by notable photographers were identified as having been chemically treated to intensify the images. In the opinion of the Moors, a print which has undergone intensification loses its provenance and is no longer representative of the original photographer's work. 'Visually the subject matter can be attributed to the photographer, but the print characteristics essential to the presentation of the image cannot be,' they insist. 'Image structure characteristics are an inseparable feature of one's appreciation of an image.' Referring to the scandal of the nineteenth-century photographs, they add:

The original print qualities have been lost for all time; only the image remains as a copy. These images had been sold as pristine vintage prints for very large sums of money. The effects of this discovery sent shock waves throughout the field of photographic conservation, the photographic art market, museums and private collections.

The processes which are arousing the greatest cause for concern are primarily photographic production processes. Treatments such as: intensification, stain removal, bleach and re-development and processing for permanance. These purely photographic techniques do not satisfy the standards, ethics and principles of conservation, nor do they satisfy every level of a photograph's existence, treating one material element of its stratigraphy to the detriment of the others.

The Moors maintain that applied techniques in any treatment should not in any way affect the long-term stability of the artefact. Chemical treatment by introducing irremovable chemical complexes will increase the instability of an already unstable material. 'Any increase in the interactive air surface area of silver images as with intensification or chemical cleaning techniques will render them more open and prone to attack by even the smallest levels of airborne or migratory contaminants, resulting in their renewed degradation. Renewed chemical activity during any processing results in the deposition and retention of chemically active substances within the paper base and/or emulsion, producing a very unstable material whose long-term preservation and stability is far from certain,' they say.

A final note on the photographic aspect from Don Etherington: Leaving aside the problems of chemical stability, the problems which are primarily encountered by most conservators of bound materials are those which are presented by scrapbooks and albums and those which are presented by the mounting of photographs within the text block or to the binding materials. The intrinsic association which the photographic materials have with the structure is usually the issue which has to be resolved. Decisions to remove such materials must always take into consideration why the photographs were put there in the first place and what damage will be sustained to the meaning of the artefact as a whole if they are removed. It is this curatorial/ owner's decision which is not easy.

Current guidelines suggested by many photographic conservators outline the types of materials which are compatible with photographic artefacts. Some of these may be appropriate for interleaving with a bound structure if interleaving is the selected alternative to removal. Often a bound structure will require disbinding and treatment to resolve some problem with paper support to which the photographs are attached. It may occasionally be suitable to simply replace poor quality supports with good quality supports in an album.

Meanwhile, efforts are being made to tackle future problems at source, and a wide variety of acid-free buffered and unbuffered papers are already available to publishers and printers in America and Europe (indeed, the American National Standards Institute has developed a standard for the permanence of book papers). However, although already used by some enlightened publishers, like all 'optional extras' they are slow to catch on, and one only hopes that education will eventually make the point.

Eight

PERIPHERAL AREAS: BOOKPLATES, EPHEMERA AND FINE BINDING

Collectors who are proud of their libraries may be tempted to adorn their books with a personal bookplate, notwithstanding the current obsession with 'unblemished' copies. However, since they have no intention of selling, they need not feel inhibited; if on the other hand the person is a celebrity, the plate may even add something to the book's value.

However, bibliophiles who decorate their books in this way for reasons of pride – or as a deterrent to thieves, are not necessarily interested in bookplates as such, which are collected for the same reason as the volumes they adorn – for their historical interest, their association with famous owners, their aesthetic appeal, and perhaps even a particular theme they illustrate.

Interest is at a low ebb today compared with the nineteenth century when the number of collectors reached a peak – although the practice of commissioning personal plates for private libraries had been common among those who could afford it for hundreds of years. At the beginning of the century it was still possible to buy from boxes of plates outside secondhand bookshops, in the same way as prints are stocked today; but in recent years the activity has visibly declined and I know of only one bookseller in the United Kingdom – at Berkhamsted, Herts – and none in the United States, who actually specialises in this area. Indeed, this is one reason why it has been difficult to sustain interest. The appetites of would-be collectors may be stimulated by 'teaser' pieces like this, but then they encounter the difficulties of finding a choice of plates.

However, an energetic Bookplate Society maintains that interest is growing again, despite the fact that a membership of 325 – half in the United Kingdom, and the rest overseas – seems very small compared with the vast numbers of book enthusiasts, some of whom must be potential recruits . . . which is my reason for introducing the subject. A growing awareness will in itself attract dealers – even though initially these may be collectors selling duplicates – and as soon as it becomes easier to buy, new collectors will come in. There is already a healthy interest on the Continent, and the bookplate society in Japan has over 1,000 members.

To most bibliophiles, the most surprising feature of this collecting field is the very low prices paid for plates by artists whose work in any other medium would be dramatically more expensive; this alone should be an incentive to those of us with interests in art and graphic design. Another is that most plates are purchased 'loose', which means there is seldom any conflict of interest when encountering a reasonably expensive book. In general, bookplate collectors would not buy a book priced at (say) £20, simply to obtain the plate – unless it was of exceptional interest. Similarly, when a plate of outstanding merit comes with a valuable book, the plate collector has to take a back seat. At a London auction in 1983 a rare incunable featured one of the earliest known 'Porcupine' bookplate by an unknown German artist, possibly Albrecht Durer (1471–1528). It fetched £7,500 but no one was able to estimate whether it would have been much less without the plate, and nor could there have been any question of removing the plate to be sold separately!

How do personal bookplates come on to the market? In the main, an artist/engraver designing a plate for a customer may run off, with or without permission, an extra number for sale – the precise figure depending on the potential interest. The majority of these designs, often very attractive, sell for under £1, but even 'fashionable' artists do not command prices commensurate with their talents. An ordinary wood engraving by Eric Gill will be worth £100 or more; the same illustration as a bookplate is worth no more than £20. A rare illustrated bookplate design by Aubrey Beardsley can fetch up to £50, yet one that is relatively common is worth only £5. Plates by Rex Whistler sell between £5–£15. 'Unfinished' designs, like proof copies of books, are worth more because they are more unusual, but there are few other direct comparisons with book prices.

One would have thought, for example, that limited editions commemorating some special event would appreciate in the same way as books, but this is not so, e.g. after the Coronation of King Edward VII in 1902, fifty sets of three 'Royal' plates were printed and sold for the benefit of the King's Hospital Fund. The three using a permutation of the Royal Arms, Garter, Crest and Imperial Crown, were priced at £8/8s, which was a lot of money in those days when interest in bookplates was at a peak; yet although they seldom appear as a set the estimated price today would in the region of only £20, possibly more on the art market. Coincidentally, the present Prince of Wales was approached shortly after his marriage to see if he would repeat that Royal precedent by allowing his own bookplate to be used for the same purpose (i.e. for the charity he sponsored) but after serious consideration he declined because he considered his own, designed by Joan Hassall, was 'too personal'.

I became aware of historical bookplates through my interest in Samuel Pepys, who took pride in his books and liked to show them off. He commissioned five – two portraits and two heraldic (both styles most commonly used in the early days), and another with his initials, S.P. against a background of Admiralty crossed anchors. In his diary entry for 21 July 1668, he reports spending 'about an hour, contriving my little plates for my books', while on the 27th of the same month he added: 'This day my plate-maker comes with my four little plates for the four yards, cost me £5; which troubles me but yet doth please me also.'

The first bookplate is believed to have been designed by one of three German artists, probably Durer, considered by many to be the outstanding German artist of the Renaissance in Northern Europe, who did a number of outstanding plate 'portraits' of the book collectors of the day. It would make him the first of many distinguished artists over the centuries to lend their talents in this direction; bookplate design requires special skills – it is not a question of using any design and simply reducing it to size! The earliest English engraved plate followed about fifty years later, in 1574.

Separate categories of design seemed to follow in chronological sequence. Since the first users were mainly aristocrats and gentry who had their coats-of-arms printed from copper engravings, they became known as 'Early Armorials'. 'Jacobean' and 'Chippendale', which followed in the eighteenth and early nineteenth centuries, had progressively elaborate designs as the names imply, the latter being especially ornate. Later came the grand landscape pictorial scene inspired by Thomas Bewick, and finally an illustrative style which encompassed most forms of artistic expression in a variety of moods.

Some of the great collections of the past have been bequeathed to museums, and have become invaluable works of reference – such as that of Sir Wollaston Franks whose 80,000 bookplates became the basis of the British Museum collection now standing at some 200,000. Somewhat weak in his coverage of certain countries, Franks was particularly strong on Britain and the United States, and the catalogues for these two countries alone occupies three large volumes.

However, this and similar collections are modest by today's standards as the bookplates of other countries have become available. Anything under 15,000 is considered small; 15,000–40,000 medium, and over 40,000 large. But that of Professor William Elliott Butler, an American Professor of Comparative Law living in London, and fomer Hon Secretary of the Bookplate Society, runs into six figures, which must be one of the largest in private hands. His main interests are aesthetic and bibliographic.

Bookseller James Wilson, of Berkhamsted, Herts, is a bookplate collector who happens to sell them, as opposed to the other way about. In 1987 he was contemplating retirement from his bookdealing activities to concentrate on plates, and was already 'stocking up' in preparation. At one London auction he purchased two collections totalling 20,000 items which were added to his existing collection of 60,000. Among them were 1,000 erotic bookplates, many designed by artists of outstanding talent, such as Franz von Bayros, the rococo artist who, as well as illustrating books, made over 300 bookplates (see my *Browser's Guide to Erotica*, David & Charles 1981); another in the modern school is Michael Fingesten, represented by a hundred designs in considerable demand. Coincidentally, at an auction of erotic bookplates in Belgium in 1986, copper impressions of works by von Bayros were fetching £25–£30, considered expensive by most

English enthusiasts, yet something very similar offered in an art gallery would fetch several hundreds of pounds.

Mr Wilson recalls the first plate he ever sold – to a young woman who selected a dozen or so 'armorials', which can usually be bought very cheaply (at the time under £1 apiece). Asked if she was a collector, she seemed surprised, and when it transpired that her sole interest was in 'pussycats', he realised that she had merely selected armorials featuring heraldic lions and other wild cats. But among the collectors he knows is one who is interested in anything which includes an elephant in the design; another Oxford and Cambridge college plates; yet another in Don Quixote, of which the owner already has hundreds.

His own collection has two main facets – the work of artists of quality and imagination: Hogarth, Vertue, Bewick, Blake, Pisaro (Lucian), Kate Greenaway, Eric Gill, Paul Nash and Oscar Kokosschka, and those of famous people – Royalty and world leaders, including Hitler, Mussolini, F. D. Roosevelt, and show business celebrities. Duplicates go into stock, and these vary from the very cheap to the occasional rare item such as the first British plate to have the engraver's signature (William Marshall) which is worth £50.

Bookplates are only seldom bought with their book, and then usually from inexpensive stock or jumble sales, but occasionally collectors strike lucky such as the occasion when the secondhand department of Blackwell's of Oxford had on their 50p shelves part of the Dennis Wheatley library, i.e. the reprints and paperbacks. The books were only worth the asking price but inside each was an unknown plate designed for the author by the brilliant artist Frank Pape. The plate was interesting not only because of the artist but because of the unusual occult theme featuring Wheatley in a garden next to a friend who was later murdered!

The present Bookplate Society has its origins in the Ex-Libris Society, formed in 1891, but being wound up seventeen years later. In 1972 it was re-launched in association with the Private Libraries Association, with a modest but growing membership until it was able to become independent in 1982. In the course of a year, members receive quarterly newsletters, two journals and a complimentary copy of a relevant book; in 1987, for example, it was on Franz von Bayros.

In the introduction I described dust jackets as the ephemera of yesterday. Today, books and jackets are so closely linked that we seldom think of them as separate entities any more. The same assumption may be applied to a large slice of today's ephemera, where the borders between a book (bodies such as UNESCO have attempted to define a book as a printed work in excess of thirty-two pages), and so-called 'fringe material' is somewhat blurred.

As book people, most of us cannot enthuse over old soup or beer labels, while regarding political broadsides and pamphlets, Acts of Parliament, letters and postcards, or even early theatre and film posters, as merely different expressions of the written word, and as such 'extensions' of the book or magazine. Admittedly, there are grey areas, but to deny the principle is to argue that manuscripts, diaries, or any pre-published material should not be classified as books. The only fundamental difference is that a book or diary is meant to be kept, but ephemera represents the minor *transient* documents of everyday life.

My curiosity must be widely shared because activity in the field has expanded considerably since 1975 when The Ephemera Society – its first President, appropriately John Betjeman – was formed in an attempt to bring some order into what is by definition a rambling and somewhat chaotic market. Apart from bringing together collectors, dealers and other interested parties, through its quarterly journal, it informs and educates.* In other words, the society is concerned with the preservation, study and educational uses of printed and handwritten ephemera of everyday life. It also acts as a clearing house and repository for items. Eventually it is hoped to set up a permanent archive, and plans also include the initiating of research and educational projects.

As booklovers, our interest does not generally extend to the other aspects of collecting ephemera, such as paper fans and paper or plastic cups – among a broad range of products produced

*A Notes & Queries page deals with questions like:
Q: I have a bill from 'John Vetch, Grocer, at the sign of the Three Sugar Loaves, the fourth door from the Minories, Al(d)gate' dated 30 July 1772 itemising the goods sold. Among the sugar and tea appears the item 'Harts horn Shavings'. What on earth were Harts horn Shavings and what were they used for?
A: The answer can be found in *The Kitchen in History*, by Molly Harrison, 1972. . . . In short [my abbreviation] a paste made from the shavings of deer's antlers and spirits of wine and milk, and used for cleaning table silver.

'specifically for short-term use, and generally for disposal'. Admittedly, an artefact does not have to be printed to throw light on a given subject, as the HRC of the University of Texas has shown in re-creating the studies of celebrated writers, complete down to pipe and slippers. Maurice Rickards, writer and designer, who founded the society and is currently Vice-President, has for the past ten years been engaged on compiling an *Encyclopaedia of Ephemera*, which will have 500 main category headings. An ordinary entry would be 500 words, but major subjects, such as posters, might run to 8,000 words.

Graham Hudson, another Council member, writing in the *Antiquarian Book Monthly Review* (Sept 1986), suggests that the collector casts his net 'so wide . . . that all human life is there . . .' He goes on: 'The study of ephemera can thus illuminate so much, touching on everything from turnpike tickets to airline route maps, from eighteenth century birth control devices to modern packaging for the pill.

Broadly, ephemerists approach collecting in either of two ways. One is where the collection relates to the material *form*, e.g. tradesmen's cards, early magazines, or advertising insets. The other is where collecting focuses on a theme, e.g. railway history, costume or education, in which case the emphemera will be perceived as but one aspect of a great whole, wherein both artefacts and books will be included.'

Enthusiasts like Maurice Rickards question ingrained attitudes; asking that if a person interested in social history, collects a period laundry list it should not make any difference if that list is handwritten – or printed. That should make us think, because all bibliophiles of my acquaintance would instinctively throw the latter away.

However, to return to 'literary' bygones, a growing number of bookdealers are taking stands at ephemera fairs and bazaars which are generally worth a visit, if only for the novelty aspect – the unfamiliar variety of material and the fact that because there are no auction records to set precedents, prices can vary, sometimes to the buyers' advantage. Similarly, there is enough material of a bookish nature to attract the type of person who would want to read this book. Academic works, for example, give us the bare bones of social history, but it is the disposable 'loose' documentation – the 'ragged edge' – broadsides, posters and handbills, not often available through scholarly sources at the time, which bring those skeletal figures to life.

There are often items of surprisingly direct interest to the bibliophiles, such as book *labels,* supplied from the early days of printing by binders, circulating libraries, etc. In common with bookplate collectors, the ephemera enthusiast can also strike lucky browsing through shelves in a bookshop for home-made bookmarks which might in their own right be of particular interest. In most cases booksellers will allow them to remove such material which in normal circumstances would be thrown away.

The Ephemera Society holds an annual exhibition on a given theme, initially in London and afterwards in other centres. In 1983 it was 'Crime and Punishment' and as a souvenir of that occasion, Maurice Rickards compiled a fascinating insight into the sociological injustices of the past. Included is an example of the execution broadsheet, a familiar sight in major cities of the eighteenth and nineteenth centuries which conducted public hangings. Printed well in advance of the execution they still managed, with a great deal of journalistic imagination (anticipating the modern yellow press), not only to describe the hanging – but also report the victim's dying speech! Another fascinating exhibit was an 1847 reward poster promising £300 for information about an attempt to rob a Lombard Street Letter Carrier – the postman of the day. It seems that because of their regular routine, postmen were constantly being attacked and robbed – to the extent that users of the service would try to reduce the risks by mailing banknotes in two halves on successive days, although apparently the robbers soon worked that one out!

A bookseller who keeps a large stock of ephemera at his two-floor shop in Chester, is Iain Campbell, who tends to specialise in eighteenth- and nineteenth-century printed matter. The sort of thing that interests him and which he can easily sell the moment they become available are Game Licences for the Lake District, signed by Wordsworth in his capacity as a local magistrate. He has also found a growing demand for single sheet advertising inserts used in nineteenth-century journals – particularly for those promoting pre-1850 Ordnance Survey maps. The sheets were either thrown away immediately, or when the journals were assembled and bound, but those surviving today provide a useful reference tool for dating old maps. One of these giveaways today fetches £8–£10 in good condition; indeed, early pull-out advertisements on a variety of subjects are collectable, especially when in colour.

Old banknotes are something else which could turn up at a ephemera stall, although collectors specialising in this narrow interest would generally deal with firms like Spink & Co, coin dealers since 1666. I recall seeing a film comedy about a £1M note (starring Gregory Peck), but in fact they were actually produced, although never issued, in 1948 when the Bank of England printed eleven of them. For some reason there was a sudden change of heart and ten were destroyed, and the remaining one cancelled and given to a senior bank official as a retirement souvenir. On his death his family sold it. In 1982 it changed hands again for £16,000, but today it would be worth considerably more. Even small denomination notes (in fine condition) have appreciated in spectacular fashion. £1 notes minted on the outbreak of the World War in 1914 when there was a threat of a run on gold, today fetch up to £1,000, and £1 notes overprinted with a Dardanelles stamp for use by troops in that campaign would be worth up to £2,500 in mint condition.

Many bibliophiles are reluctant to get involved because of the unfamiliarity of collating so many 'bits and pieces', even though most ephemerists tend to concentrate on one or two themes. Items are generally mounted, filed in boxes, and stocked on horizontal 'slots' in place of shelves. An area of interest that would appeal to me, for example, might be broadsides. Ken Leach, the Vermont bookseller already mentioned, makes a speciality of gathering old and often unrecorded material, and subsequently selling it as a collection. He did this, for example, with a collection of seventeen broadsides dating from 1766–1865 on the theme of American transport (i.e. stagecoach, railroad, river boats and steam packets), and at his asking price of $5,200 could have sold them several times over.

It is obvious that the more a dealer puts himself about, the greater his chances of success, and Ken is typical of the beavers who never give up and deserve their success rate. In 1980 he bought from a 'picker' (i.e. an upmarket rag and bone man who

172

goes from door to door hoping to buy anything old from attics and barns, usually antiques) eight eighteenth-century pamphlets, including two items (one the 1792 Vermont State Constitution) which lacked their last leaves. Two months later Ken went to an estate auction about seventy-five miles away, and in the bottom of a box of old cookbooks, he found two more pamphlets – and the missing leaves of his original purchase!

Although it has only 700 members (including institutional bodies) in the UK, the society is growing on an international scale, with an offshoot organisation in the United States with a similar number of members and in 1987 opening others in Australia and Canada.

Mention the craft of binding to the average book collector and he thinks instinctively, and somewhat guiltily, of the old family bible that needs rebacking or the covers repaired . . . when the money can be spared. Few of us think of the binder as a creative artist, or are aware of the strides made in bookbinding design during the past thirty years. I admit to being a little prejudiced because in researching *Fine Bookbinding in the Twentieth Century* (David & Charles 1984) I got to know a number of very talented designer binders, the majority of whom still having to supplement their income by other means, usually teaching.

Yet the irony is that (apart from collections in libraries and museums) most modern bindings are commissioned or bought at exhibitions by bibliophiles – as opposed to art collectors – despite the fact that these *objets d'art* are not' purchased to read. The twentieth century has seen a renaissance in fine binding, which has considerably extended the horizons of an old craft, principally in aesthetic terms but also through a whole new approach to the work. There is an upsurge in standards which had been allowed to slip for so many years, but the main difference in philosophy of the modern school is that, in addition to structural and functional considerations, binders see their role as providing in the book's cover an extension of the author's 'message'.

There was a time when popular stock designs could be bought off the peg in the same way as fabric patterns, with binders slavishly copying what was the vogue irrespective of the book's contents. Now binders interpret their brief in a variety of styles, illustrative and abstract, by the use of the whole spectrum of colour and even by the use of different materials. On the other hand, there are brilliant craftsmen who believe that the role of each contributor to the construction of a book, i.e. typographer and binder, as well as author is equal. But both 'schools' agree that the creative binding should stand as an art object in its own right, and not just as an appendage in afterthought.

If binders charged for their time, as do people in the professions, then few of us could afford to buy (actually a handful at the 'top' end of the market are in a privileged position where on the strength of international reputations, they can); but most fix an arbitrary price which is seldom expensive for something unique, and which will almost certainly appreciate in value. The private collector is usually able to display his chosen masterpiece, but libraries and institutions fortunate enough to have collections representative of modern binding are obliged to keep them in their hand-crafted protective boxes, which are usually fairly plain. Occasionally the box is also decorated in some way but even that has to be limited, or else they too would need to be housed in protective boxes!

There are so many different qualities that need to be incorporated into a fine binding, of course, and it does not have to be dazzlingly eye-catching; in fact the works of some of the outstanding craftsmen in the world today seem quite unspectacular at first glance. Jean de Gonet, for example, broke new ground by insisting that the design should not emanate from the story content but from the basic structure of the book, which to him means the cords . . . and that reminds me of another binding by Trevor Jones, described by a reviewer at a Crafts Council exhibition in 1985, as 'subtle' when he had seen only *half* the design – because the binding had been incorrectly displayed with the covers closed instead of open.

What is interesting about this misconception is that the binding for James Joyce's *Fragments* was commissioned by Duval and Hamilton, booksellers specialising in modern binding, who had commissioned him to do one for the same title ten years before for a major exhibition *British Bookbinding Today* – bought in its entirety by the Lilly Library, Indiana. As with all Trevor's work, the first version had been highly original, incorporating an assemblage of jetsam and leather objects picked up from beaches along the coast of North West England, because it seemed to him that the re-use

174

and re-fashioning of fragments of discarded artefacts was a reasonable parallel to the way Joyce was reshaping language in the chapters of what was to become *Finnegans Wake*. For the second, he felt there should be 'an unmistakably family relationship' between the two. However, he decided that this time the design should come from the leather doublures (the inside face of the covers), with only faint peripheral traces 'escaping through' to the outer covers – the fragments which appears on the outside leather being extensions of the inner designs.

Trevor's willingness to experiment with the medium – although never at the expense of the binding's integrity – was a contributory factor to the early recognition of his talent (although he was not able to give up lecturing and bind full-time until 1985). He was, for example, one of the pioneers of treating leathers with certain types of dye to create interesting visual and textual effects.

Another brilliant craftsman who made his mark initially with an 'experimental' design using electronics as a feature of a perspex and metal binding with working parts – but who has subsequently proved to be perhaps the most versatile of the younger creative binders, is James Brockman, President of the Designer Bookbinders from 1985–7. Despite a conventional 'apprenticeship', Brockman's appropriately revolutionary binding for Philip Smith's *New Directions in Bookbinding* was sensational enough to disturb some of the more traditional elements, causing them to brand him as 'the engineer binder', but he was able to counter those claims by successive demonstrations of his artistic abilities, and such intricate craftsman's skill as gold tooling.

Currently, Brockman is working in two entirely different directions. More interesting from the aesthetic viewpoint, is the staining of transparent vellum, using a spirit dye under the vellum, and combining this effect with gold tooling and onlays (pieces of leather laid on top, as opposed to 'inlays', which are set-in). His recent binding for *Comus* incorporating these ideas was a prize winner at the 1985 Prix Paul Bonet competition in Switzerland. The other line, fascinating to the more technically minded is an extension of his researches when producing his two earlier metal/electronic bindings, which featured specially designed hinges to allow the boards to open as fully as any leather binding. On those occasions he had designed and made a double hinge for each board

175

– resulting in four hinges or joints for each book. Since then he has been striving to perfect a single-hinge binding, a remarkably complex task. The first has already been exhibited, and when he is satisfied he can progress no further, he will consider a wooden version! 'There is nothing new in using metal for binding,' he explains, 'but I consider experimenting with modern and traditional materials to be part of the natural evolution of bookbinding. It is possible to go down many a blind alley before achieving satisfactory results but we must look to the future and evolve new methods while remembering always our long and proven traditions.'

Most professional binders are wary of 'artists' on the fringe, whose ideas of free expression are not supported by the necessary craft skills – those on what might be called ego trips who lose sight of the purpose of a binding and come up with weird attachments and gimmicks that even prevent the book from being handled. Nevertheless, in trying to extend the boundaries of modern binding, responsible bodies such as the Designer Bookbinders have been influencing the work of students with an annual competition – allowing them a looser rein which does not stifle their natural creativity. In the latest competition, two of the most interesting entries were a binding made for a *Bicycle Company Visitor's Book*, made from spokes, brake-blocks, chains, metal and rubber; and for a book of World War I poems, *The Pity of War*, which had a design resembling a stitched wound, liberally sprinkled with iodine. To the best of James Brockman's knowledge, it was the first modern binding to incorporate a smell!

The trouble is that many of these innovative students will choose other careers in art, because interest in fine binding is so limited that most hand binders could not survive on this work alone. However, this is not the place to develop the argument. I merely urge bibliophiles to take a closer look at modern fine binding whenever there is an exhibition in their town or city. There are almost as many design concepts as there are in dust jackets, and the extra dimension turns many of them into works of art. The alternative is to contact the London headquarters of the international body of Designer Bookbinders; the Crafts Council in London, both of which have directories of talented craftspersons, with slides as examples, and information on where their work can be seen; or even the HRC at Austin which is opening a binding school.

Nine

CRIME AND PUNISHMENT

There is no argument over defining the verb 'to steal'; nor that theft is a crime. Yet as soon as we apply the judgement to books, the waters become muddied. Obviously, someone who deliberately takes a book from a shop or library is engaged in a criminal act – although there seems to be some moral code that stealing from a large bookstore or chain is less reprehensible than robbing the corner shop where the owner may be known as a 'good guy' trying to earn a crust.

It is not uncommon for students to appropriate text books in this way, but what about those who steal from their own college library? One large English university library has had in the region of 1,300 books 'missing' at any one time – despite standard security measures. The problem is that students have to be given access to routine research material (manuscripts are kept under supervision), and short of a body search every time they leave the library, there is not much that can be done, without changing moral attitudes. The librarian concerned is convinced that in most cases the books taken are genuinely needed, and that the borrower is either desperate because of academic pressures, or feels that he/she has a *right* to hang on to that book for the duration! Libraries housing rare books, and catering for outside researchers, obviously have to be much stricter, and some like the HRC in Texas have video cameras and a battery of monitors that would do credit to a major security operation.

'Borrowing' books is a more ambiguous area. With or without permission, borrowing a book from a friend, and 'forgetting' to return it – may not be a criminal act, but it is *cheating* which is morally as bad. While I despise cranks who talk about the corrupting influence of books (when they mean they disagree with the writer's views), I wonder what it is about a book, even the cheapest paperback, that makes ordinary, decent people sink to such levels when they would not dream of doing the same with a print, or a piece of pottery – or even an ashtray. Many years ago, before I learned not to deface books, I was able to lend, having my name neatly stamped inside the front cover. Today it is simpler not to bother unless one has a spare copy.

The traditional theft, i.e. shoplifting, is generally the work of a bibliophile, although occasionally others succumb to the temptation – such as the man who stole from a famous West End antiquarian booksellers to pay for his girl friend's abortion. Many dealers of my acquaintance have been misled by a customer's appearance, carefully watching the shabby individual, and ignoring the scholarly 'gentleman' – to their cost. However, in recent years, book theft has moved into the area of organised crime, which means that when the crooks are determined enough, even the move to more secure upstairs showrooms, will not keep them out. Indeed people operating on this level have come a long way since 1977 when burglars dropped through the skylight of a London shop to pull-off the bulkiest book-theft of all time – using a van or lorry to make off with a few thousand volumes. Now shops are easy targets for the burglar, while the more intelligent crook realises that the tougher the break-in the higher the likely rewards.

Barry R. Levin, the SF specialist, who now operates from offices with show space, suffered from the ingenuity of thieves despite the usual store security devices. Having shown a recent prize acquisition – the *Lord of the Rings* trilogy (first editions in dust jackets and a letter from Tolkein) – to a fellow Los Angeles dealer just before closing, for once he did not put them in the safe, but left them in a locked case with the shop motion detector switched on. But during the night, thieves broke in, drilled the case from the rear to avoid the detector, and escaped not only with the Tolkein but several other rare items. Next morning he reported the theft. Weeks later another SF bookstore had a break-in and a number of special books taken, followed by an attempted burglary at a third store – this time in Sherman Oaks. After that incident the men were arrested, photographed and fingerprinted – but released through lack of evidence. However, the owner of the bookstore mentioned the incident to the author Harlan Ellison, who contacted the Los Angeles police advising them of a possible connection. When they obtained 'mug shots' from their colleagues in Sherman Oaks, and showed them (with unrelated photographs) to Barry Levin, he was able to identify one of the suspects, whose house was searched and a hoard of stolen books found. As Barry recalls 'If it were not for Harlan Ellison's quick thinking, the case might never have been solved. Our burglar turned out, much to my dismay, to be a good customer. At the time he was arrested, we were holding several hundred dollars worth of books for him!'

In the United Kingdom, thefts from bookshops which are likely to be discovered quickly have more chance of being recovered if only because the Antiquarian Booksellers Association operates a very efficient telephone chain system – even extended to reputable booksellers who do not belong to the association – warning them to be on the lookout for the stolen items. Since setting up a Books Security Committee some fifteen years ago, it has also forged useful links with the police, although the relationship did suffer a setback when the Arts Squad, which was beginning to understand the special characteristics of book thefts, was disbanded after police decided that the fight against violent crimes should take precedence. There are hopeful signs that intensive lobbying by the ABA will result in the squad being reformed in the not too distant future.

Commenting on the committee's success in general, Roger Bayntun-Williams, a map and print specialist, who acts as liaison with the police, says 'A well known petty crook stole a suitcase from the feet of the owner who was buying a rail ticket at a main line station. The thief could not have known that the contents of the case was a collection of Sheridan memorabilia, ephemera and annotated books, an irreplaceable collection which was being returned from exhibition in London. The theft was reported to the ABA late in the evening. The thief was charged with the theft at 11am the following morning, having tried to sell the books to a dealer who had already been warned by phone. Thieves are regularly caught because they suppose no one will know of the theft.'

Of course when the books come from a library where their disappearance may not be noticed for some time, the odds are

179

greater and much depends on the vigilance of individual booksellers. Rare books worth £1M stolen from University College, London, were recovered after collaboration between Scotland Yard, Interpol and the United States customs agents – following a tip-off by the manager at Quaritch suspicious of someone trying to sell him valuable books from a suitcase. The mysterious vendor, a 'Dr French', was in fact a Greek-born graduate student of Columbia University, who left two of the books behind as a show of good faith; the library stamps had been bleached out. The police were contacted, but the man did not return for his books. In due course the U.S. customs officials set-up an undercover operation in which a Manhattan rare book dealer agreed to meet the suspect over lunch to discuss the purchase of some books. He was even provided with a bullet-proof waistcoat! The man was arrested at the conclusion of lunch, and a score of other stolen books were found at his flat.

Another academic who had not set his sights so high, stole 281 books worth a mere £14,000 from an Oxford college over an eighteen-month period; an eighteen-month prison sentence seems an apt reward! Public libraries are even more vulnerable, although books there are seldom valuable. One public library reported annual losses of not less than £10,000 – which new security equipment immediately reduced to £300. Even so, a ratepayer was reported as objecting to the system on the grounds of the 'invasion of privacy'.

Discussing the different types of thief, Roger Bayntun-Williams says: 'A school teacher who stole books as a protest against the profit bookshops were making did not gain a lot of sympathy; nor the man who stole some 5,000 library books for his personal library. A man living in a chicken shed with a small collection of books might – provided the books are not yours!'

So much petty crime while deplorable might be explained, even justified as in the case of a starving person stealing food. Most bibliophiles can understand the temptation of a desirable book that for one reason or another cannot be purchased. But pointless vandalism, tearing up of flowers in a public park, or smashing public telephones – is seldom punished severely enough. Books are stolen but seldom vandalised; ironically the most spectacular case of defacing books which came to a British court in 1962 was not only severely punished – but did actually have some point, apart from being 'creatively' carried out.

The crime was perpetrated by playwright Joe Orton and his lover Kenneth Halliwell; five years later Halliwell murdered Orton and then committed suicide. The story of their ill-fated relationship is recounted in John Lahr's *Prick Up Your Ears* (Allen Lane 1978), but my interest here is confined to their relationship with Islington Borough Libraries, a battle of wits in the true sense – because it took a measure of ingenuity to catch the pair.

The charge sheet* at London's Old Street Magistrates Court gave little hint of the scale of their eighteen-month operation. What emerged was that the plates were used to paper the walls, floor to ceiling, of their bed-sitter, while others were used to 'decorate' an assortment of dust jackets which were then returned to the shelves (so that the reactions of other borrowers could be observed!) It was the eye-catching defacement of the dust jackets more than anything else which tickled the imagination of the popular press and resulted in headlines. The pair were sent to prison for six months, and ordered to pay costs which, since they never had any money at that stage of Orton's career – rubbed salt into the wounds. In retrospect one wonders whether a few years later when Orton was a major figure in theatre, if that sentence would not have been suspended and substituted by a hefty fine which he could have paid with indifference.

As it was, prison may well have been the experience which crystalised Orton's writing potential. It transformed him from a young man on the point of despair with rejection notes which acknowledged his writing talent but complained of plot inadequacy, into a playwright of rare originality. By then he had work accepted by the BBC, but his writing had no direction and on the charge sheet he was described as a 'lens cleaner'. Certainly he had little doubt, telling the Leicester *Mercury* in 1964, '. . . Being in the nick brought detachment to my writing,' and the magazine *Plays & Players*, a year later '. . . Brought me the revelation of what really lies beneath an industrial society.'

The story of the successful prosecution was told by Alexander Connell, Chief Librarian at Islington's Central Lending Library,

*Stealing 72 library books and wilfully damaging a number of books including the removal of 1,653 plates from art books . . . total damage estimated at £450.

181

in the March 1963 edition of *The Library Association Record*. The discovery of books in a multilated condition was nothing unusual, he pointed out; but it was soon realised that the damage was not sporadic. Listing the categories of defacement, he refers first to the addition of false blurbs typewritten on the jackets of Gollancz detective fiction. 'The choice of this publisher for this type of operation was a cunning one,' he states. 'Many . . . are designed in a "dashed-off" manner, and the typewritten matter blended so well with the style of the jackets that one did not realise they were additions. These false blurbs were also couched in a literary style usual in such composition and it was not until one had read the complete blurb that what the judge termed "amusing or mildly obscene" wording made its impact.'

In fact, Mr Connell understandably gives Orton little credit for the ingenuity of his prose, and it is unfortunate that so few of the mock Gollancz jackets survive. (Islington Library has a collection of the 'montage' effect jackets, but only one of these.) Typical, however, was this blurb for *Clouds of Witness*, by Dorothy Sayers:

When little Betty Macdree says that she has been interfered with, her mother at first laughs. It is only something that the kiddy had picked up off television. But when sorting through the laundry, Mrs Macdree discovers that a new pair of knickers are missing she thinks again. On being questioned, Betty bursts into tears. Mrs Macdree takes her to the police station and to everyone's surprise the little girl identifies WPC Brenda Coolidge as her attacker. Brenda a new recruit, denies the charge. A search is made of the Women's Police Barracks. What is found there is a seven inch phallus and a pair of knickers of the kind used by Betty. All looks black for kindly WPC Collidge . . . What can she do? This is one of the most enthralling stories ever written by Miss Sayers.

It is the only one in which the murder weapon is concealed, not for reasons of fear but for reasons of decency!

READ THIS BEHIND CLOSED DOORS. And have a good shit while you are reading!

The irony, from the collector's point of view, is that early first editions of Dorothy Sayers are in increasing demand, especially with dust jackets – something I could never understand. *Clouds of*

Witness, only her second mystery was originally published in 1926 by Fisher Unwin without one, so the Gollancz edition was a reprint but complete with the Orton one-off defacement would be worth £500, or more. Surely anyone going from Orton's refreshing style (conceding that perhaps his last line is slightly 'over the top'), to the first page in which Lord Peter Wimsey is addressed by his butler with such scintilating dialogue as 'Good Morning, my Lord. Fine morning, my Lord. Your Lordship's bath-water is ready,' must have felt let down.

Part of Orton's 'kick' was in gauging the effect of his work. In an interview quoted by John Lahr, he says: 'When I put the plastic covers back over the jacket, you couldn't tell that the blurbs weren't printed. I would stand in corners after I'd smuggled the doctored books back into the library, and then watch the people read them. It was very funny, very interesting.'

But a far more eye-catching category were paste-and-scissors jobs on dust jackets which (under the plastic covers) would pass for normal at first glance; a double-take would reveal their incongruity. Some were garish – an historical theme on *Queen's Favourite* transformed by wrestling homosexuals on the front and similar incongruities on the back. Others were more subtle – the addition of a small penis, for example stuck in a natural position, would have been missed by most browsers. There were monkey's faces in the centre of a beautiful flower; a tattooed man in place of a more dignified figure; photos of a man, woman and cat replacing the illustration for *Three Faces of Eve*.

'It seemed obvious that one person or group of persons was responsible,' reports Mr Connell, 'but no clue was forthcoming as to who it was until operations were switched from the central to a branch library. This played into our hands. In a heavily used central library the large number of readers prevents close observation being kept. But in the smaller traffic of a branch library it was possible to observe individual readers more closely and to notice which possible culprits had been in the library before 'finds' were made. Evenually the branch librarian found her suspicions centring round two men who shared the same address and who always visited the library together.'

At this stage the police were consulted, and on their advice, 'unknown' assistants from other departments were posted as browsing readers at the times when the two men were changing their books – but after several weeks the library was despairing of catching them. What Mr Connell then casually dismisses with the bland words, 'We contrived to obtain a sample of typewritten matter done on a machine belonging to one of the two men', was in effect the master stroke in the cat and mouse game. It hinged on a trick letter written by the borough council's solicitor accusing the suspected men of being responsible for an abandoned car which the council was prepared to remove. Its authoritarian tone sparked off an indignant response from Kenneth Halliwell, using the typewriter on which Orton had composed his blurbs; a fact established in the police forensic laboratory.

Mr Connell subsequently visited the flat, discovered that book plates completely covered the walls, trimmed and fitted to present an unbroken expanse of illustration. He estimated that more than 2,000 had been used, but since it is not the library's policy to stamp plates on the front there was no proof of ownership (short of trying to remove them which would have been impractical), but there also were more than 1,600 loose plates, many of which with the library stamp on the reverse. Then followed a slow and tedious operation by the staff to identify all the plates, consulting other libraries and publishers, a problem complicated by the fact that so many had been cut into pieces.

Neither culprit ever expressed any contrition; indeed Orton in the year of his death, interviewed by the London Evening News, declared his hatred for the library system, which he claimed from the time he asked for Gibbon's *Decline and Fall of the Roman Empire* and found it was not immediately available: 'Libraries might as well not exist; they've got endless shelves of rubbish and hardly any space for good books.' Which brings us full circle from my earlier remarks about the irrational conception of the people who have grudges against libraries . . .

POSTSCRIPT

If there is a moral in what has been revealed over the preceding chapters, it might be that knowledge is everything, that we should learn as much as we can . . . back our own judgement . . . and never put off until tomorrow what we can do today. You may have heard that before somewhere, but in book collecting terms it means that the title you are agonising over today may not be there tomorrow, or may be considerably more expensive; that the old bible you have been meaning to get repaired may be disintegrating faster than you realise. That is an alarming fact, but if you still need a carrot, let me offer the story of the French bible dating from 1600 being restored by Bernard Middleton. Removing the old leather binding, he discovered some ninety sixteenth-century playing cards lining the boards; they were presented to the bible's owner who found they were worth a *lot* of money! As we've repeatedly seen, one never knows what will turn up inside an old binding . . .

But what of the future? Speculation about books, in the year 2001 is based on discernible trends in publishing and bookselling today. Technology will continue to be the foremost influence, although whether shopping by computer terminals in our own homes comes sooner or later, remains to be seen. It may merely be a question of where we live, because the feasibility is already established – in France, for example, subscribers to a system pioneered by the national telephone network have access to a variety of facilities, growing all the time.

Elsewhere I have anticipated the literary loss to posterity as the word-processor replaces the writer's notepad and manuscript; something which is already happening. Still further in the future, the ultimate disappearance of the book itself is a real possibility. The word-processor linked into a computer network dispenses with the need for a publisher. An author could transmit his lastest novel direct to anyone prepared to feed it into his own machine.

185

Obviously, that is a sweeping over-simplification, but the concept is valid, and even the potential audience can be identified by computer. Contrast the speed and simplicity of such a link-up with the traditional publishing programme that necessitates the acquisition and storage of tons of paper, setting and printing facilities, and staffing and general overheads spanning an antiquated production cycle of up to a *year*!

Mind you, all scientific breakthroughs in history have brought problems as well as benefits. I once read a SF story about the chaos resulting from a computer malfunction in a future world in which people can no longer understand simple arithmetic. It seemed far-fetched at the time, but think for a moment of the impact in recent years of the pocket calculator, and how many of us rely on it for the simplest sums?

Obviously books will survive, if only because they are more durable than tapes. One of the principal attractions of an audio or video recorder is the 'erase' button which encourages variety, but persuades us to keep only what we consider (at that moment) the most important programme. And the loss of so much future literature will have an effect similar to that when the telephone call superceded letters as the most common means of communication – depriving us of so much invaluable evidence of history in the making.

It could be said that we collect too much rubbish; but at least we still have a choice in what we retain. There might be a time when virtually nothing survives long enough to collect. And in such a society, the antiquarian book will be sought after by a different kind of collector – the sort who would regard it not so much as a book, but an *objet d'art*, like an old painting or piece of furniture.

There is even speculation in some circles about future computers which would enable society to dispense with writers. Computers have already been programmed to remember and select the best of a number of appropriate word-structures and phrases; ultimately more sophisticated models could produce stories based on the input of a simple plot outline, which – as any viewer of soap operas will confirm – does not need the services of a creative writer. Depressing for tomorrow's authors, perhaps, but it should not worry collectors; after all, a first edition is a first edition, irrespective of what the author looks like . . .

SELECTED
BIBLIOGRAPHY

Backhouse, (J). *The Illuminated Manuscript* (Phaidon, 1979)

Cockerell, (D). *Bookbinding & The Care of Books* (5th rev. paperback edn 1978)

Crane, (W). *Of the Decorative Illustration of Books Old & New*, (originally published 1896; reprinted Bracken Books, London 1984)

Fincham, (H. W). *Artists & Engravers of British & American Bookplates* (London, 1897)

Lee, (Brian North). *British Bookplates: A Pictorial History* (David & Charles, 1982)

Lewis, (Roy Harley). *Fine Bookbinding in the 20th Century* (David & Charles, 1984)

Middleton, (B). *The Restoration of Leather Bindings* (Chicago rev. edn, 1984)

Rosner, (C). *The Growth of the Dust Jacket* (Sylvan Press, 1954)

Tanselle, (G. Thomas). *Book Jackets, Blurbs & Bibliographers* (The Library (USA) 1971, June)

Weidemann, (K). *Book Jackets & Record Covers:* An International Survey 1969

INDEX

188